T0334339

Cambridge Elements ☰

Elements in Bioethics and Neuroethics
edited by
Thomasine Kushner
California Pacific Medical Center, San Francisco

THE THREE PILLARS OF ETHICAL RESEARCH WITH NONHUMAN PRIMATES

A Work Developed in Collaboration with the National Anti-Vivisection Society

L. Syd M Johnson
SUNY Upstate Medical University

Andrew Fenton
Dalhousie University

Mary Lee Jensvold
Central Washington University

CAMBRIDGE
UNIVERSITY PRESS

Shaftesbury Road, Cambridge CB2 8EA, United Kingdom

One Liberty Plaza, 20th Floor, New York, NY 10006, USA

477 Williamstown Road, Port Melbourne, VIC 3207, Australia

314–321, 3rd Floor, Plot 3, Splendor Forum, Jasola District Centre,
New Delhi – 110025, India

103 Penang Road, #05-06/07, Visioncrest Commercial, Singapore 238467

Cambridge University Press is part of Cambridge University Press & Assessment,
a department of the University of Cambridge.

We share the University's mission to contribute to society through the pursuit of education,
learning and research at the highest international levels of excellence.

www.cambridge.org
Information on this title: www.cambridge.org/9781009525053

DOI: 10.1017/9781009525046

First published 2024

A catalogue record for this publication is available from the British Library.

ISBN 978-1-009-52505-3 Hardback
ISBN 978-1-009-52502-2 Paperback
ISSN 2752-3934 (online)
ISSN 2752-3926 (print)

The Three Pillars of Ethical Research with Nonhuman Primates

A Work Developed in Collaboration with the National Anti-Vivisection Society

Elements in Bioethics and Neuroethics

DOI: 10.1017/9781009525046
First published online: November 2024

L. Syd M Johnson
SUNY Upstate Medical University

Andrew Fenton
Dalhousie University

Mary Lee Jensvold
Central Washington University

Author for correspondence: L. Syd M Johnson, johnsols@upstate.edu

Abstract: The Three Pillars (harmonization, replacement, and justice) describe an ethical path forward and away from the use of nonhuman primates in harmful research and scientific use. Conducting nonhuman primate research in an ethical way that acknowledges their moral importance requires the satisfaction of more rigorous guidelines and regulations modeled on those that apply to similarly vulnerable human subjects, especially children and incarcerated persons. This Element argues for the moral necessity of harmonizing human and nonhuman primate research ethics, regulations, and guidelines in a way that protects all primates, human and nonhuman. The authors call for the replacement of nonhuman primates in research with human-relevant methods that do not simply shift research onto other nonhuman animals, and they challenge publics, governments, and scientific communities worldwide to implement justice in the selection and use of all research subjects. This title is also available as Open Access on Cambridge Core.

Keywords: philosophy, animal ethics, human–animal studies, research ethics, primatology

ISBNs: 9781009525053 (HB), 9781009525022 (PB), 9781009525046 (OC)
ISSNs: 2752-3934 (online), 2752-3926 (print)

Contents

Foreword: In Pursuit of Ethical Research with Nonhuman
Primates   1

1 Introduction   2

2 Harmonization   17

3 Replacement   27

4 Justice   43

5 The Path Forward   50

   Notes   56

   References   62

Foreword: In Pursuit of Ethical Research with Nonhuman Primates

The use of nonhuman primates (NHPs) in research has long been a topic of profound debate. The ethical considerations surrounding their use have ignited passionate discussions among researchers, ethicists, animal welfare advocates, and the general public.[1] Yet, despite the gravity of these discussions, historical initiatives aimed at addressing the ethics of NHP research have often been overshadowed, ignored, or even co-opted by various vested interests.

The Three Pillars of Ethical Research with Nonhuman Primates emerges from a deep concern for the ethical implications of the expanding use of NHPs in biomedical research. This Element aims to shed light on the intricate ethical landscape surrounding this controversial topic and to rekindle the dialogue that has been lacking in recent discussions, with a primary focus on the United States.

One of the driving forces behind the urgency of this Element is the recent push from within the scientific community to increase the number of NHPs used in biomedical research.[2] Although the past benefits of NHP research cannot be dismissed entirely, it is disheartening to note that the ethical implications of their increasing use have not been given due consideration in the discussions or their resulting conclusions. It is our firm belief that any proposed expansion of NHP research *must* be accompanied by a thorough exploration of the ethical dimensions involved.

Fundamentally, the arguments put forth in favor of increased NHP use often rest on the assumption that NHPs lack the cognitive, emotional, and social capacities that confer special moral standing upon humans. Yet, it must not be overlooked that some NHPs – chimpanzees in particular – have been afforded special moral standing in the United States and elsewhere, and US government funding no longer supports their use in research.

When the United States ended biomedical research on chimpanzees, Francis Collins, then director of the National Institutes of Health (NIH), called chimpanzees "very special animals" deserving "special consideration." He was quick to point out that "Research with other non-human primates will continue to be valued, supported, and conducted by the NIH,"[3] thus anticipating the impact of the decision not to use chimpanzees on other NHPs. Since that time, the scientific community has dug its heels in about the necessity and importance of NHP research.[4]

But what makes chimpanzees morally different from other NHPs? Upon close examination, it becomes apparent that no strong arguments exist to conclusively demonstrate the absence of any morally relevant capacities in other primates. The scientific community must confront this critical point and thoroughly explore the ethical implications of its actions.

The Three Pillars of Ethical Research with Nonhuman Primates aims to address this issue by delving into the three foundational pillars that underpin ethical research involving NHPs: harmonization, replacement, and justice. By thoroughly examining each pillar and their interconnections, we hope to provide researchers, policymakers, ethicists, and society at large with a comprehensive understanding of the complex ethical considerations surrounding NHP research.

This Element is not intended to provide a definitive answer to the question of whether NHP research should continue or cease altogether. Rather, it serves as an impassioned and reasoned plea to reignite the conversation, to reevaluate our assumptions, and to approach NHP research with an ethical perspective. It is our hope that by doing so, we can foster a greater understanding of the ethical implications and guide the scientific community toward a more conscientious and responsible approach to research involving NHPs that prioritizes replacing them with human-relevant models.

In writing this Element, the authors have drawn upon a wide range of interdisciplinary perspectives, including bioethics, primatology, philosophy, animal welfare science, and the social sciences to present a nuanced and holistic exploration of the ethical dimensions at play. We are indebted to the many researchers, thinkers, and advocates who have contributed to this ongoing discourse, and we sincerely hope that the Element will serve as a catalyst for meaningful dialogue and positive change.

May *The Three Pillars of Ethical Research with Nonhuman Primates* provide an opportunity for much reflection, introspection, and ethical growth. Let us embark on this journey together, striving to align scientific progress with compassionate consideration of the moral complexities inherent in our interactions with our closest primate relatives.

Kenneth Kandaras
Executive Director, National Anti-Vivisection Society
August 31, 2023

1 Introduction

For centuries, nonhuman animals have been used as substitutes for humans in anatomical studies and in the pursuit of knowledge in medicine and the biological sciences (broadly construed). They have been used when experimentation with or the use of humans was prohibited by taboo or, today, when it is limited and prohibited by laws and regulations. The use of nonhuman animals in scientific research has increased in the last century as ethical and regulatory constraints on human research have increased.[5] The most significant changes occurred in the twentieth century, particularly after the Second World War, as concerns about human rights and the protection of human research subjects led regulators to intensify safeguards and, in some cases, require prior experimentation with animals to inform human research.[6] Where these safeguards have been followed they have protected many vulnerable humans from exploitation and abuse, but the burdens of protecting human research subjects have largely been borne by nonhuman animals.

Today, the nonhuman animals used for science each year number in the millions (the exact number is unknown due to irregularities in how animals used in science are counted, both in the United States and elsewhere). The science-related activities we include under the term "science" or "scientific" include diverse types of research, experimentation, testing, observation, education, and training, as well as pursuits supporting these activities, including breeding and holding animals in colonies and facilities to supply them for scientific purposes.[7] Some nonhuman animals used for scientific purposes are provided with limited protections by animal welfare regulations, and some are not protected at all. The specifics and requirements vary from country to country. Where there are regulatory protections for *humans*, they prevent nonvoluntary research and practices that intentionally inflict significant physical, emotional, and psychological pain and distress, severe harm, permanent injury, and death. But these practices are common in research with nonhuman animals and are permitted by animal welfare regulations. Within international human research regulations, and those of many countries, captive persons, including those who are incarcerated and who live in institutional settings, are largely excluded from research by regulations that protect them from exploitation. But no such protection is provided to nonhuman animals, who are held captive in research laboratories, in scientific educational and training settings, and in breeding colonies where they are forced to produce offspring destined for use in science. Additionally, some nonhuman animals – nonhuman primates (NHPs) in particular – are captured in the wild and transported like cargo over vast distances to research labs and breeding colonies.

1.1 A Focus on the Use of Nonhuman Primates

Within the law and in ethics, certain animals have been accorded special status, reflecting the ways humans and human societies value them and view them as mattering morally. In countries like the United States and various member countries of the European Union, dogs and cats are examples of such animals. This reflects the frequent unique attachments and bonds humans can have with dogs and cats, and the view that they are creatures entitled to special care, privileges, respect, and protections. The Animal Welfare Act (1966), the first law regulating the scientific use of animals in the United States, was inspired by the massive public outcry that followed when Pepper, a Pennsylvania family's beloved dalmatian, was kidnapped and sold to a biomedical research lab in New York, where she died.[8]

Nonhuman primates, including great apes like chimpanzees and gorillas and many species of monkeys, are increasingly viewed as animals who are due special consideration,[9] in part because they are among the closest evolutionary and genetic relatives to humans, and share with humans many valued traits, like intelligence and sociality. This increased attention to NHPs reflects how they have entered the public imagination as a result of the work of popular scientists like Jane Goodall and Frans de Waal. Increasingly within research regulations, there are unique and specific regulations concerning the well-being of NHPs, and when the ethics of animal use is critically discussed, there is greater attention given to them than to the many other animals used in science.

Yet, it is also because of the presumed similarities between NHPs and humans that human-directed biomedical research, and related scientific use, turns to NHPs, even if only as the last step before human experimentation.[10] Monkeys like marmosets, squirrel monkeys, macaques, baboons, and, in the not-so-distant past, chimpanzees, have been most commonly used. Nonhuman primates are used in many kinds of research, including studies of infectious diseases, brain disorders, and reproductive disorders, in vision research, and in drug and medical device development. Recently, the development of genetically engineered pigs created to produce organs for xeno-transplantation into humans has turned to NHPs, including infant baboons, as experimental xenograft recipients.[11] As the pace of scientific research has accelerated, the demand for NHPs bred for and used in research has also increased. Several countries with large-scale brain research projects are expanding their NHP breeding and research capacity.[12] In the United States alone, an estimated 75,000 NHPs were used in both 2018 and 2019 according to the most recent US Department of Agriculture data,[13] setting new records.[14] New England Primate Conservancy calculates the total reported number of NHPs held in US research facilities in 2019 as 108,526.[15] The European Commission estimates that approximately 10,000 NHPs are used annually in research in European Union member countries. However, as the scientific community builds capacity and demands more NHPs, there is ongoing debate within and outside that community about the value and necessity of using NHPs in science to model human conditions.[16]

1.2 Why Only Nonhuman Primates?

Increased critical attention to any animal use is vital, and we do not think singling out NHPs as deserving more protection than other animals is scientifically or ethically warranted. However, the focus of this Element is on harmful scientific activity involving captive NHPs, inspired in part, as noted earlier, by trends that show increasing NHP use within several areas of research that is harmful to these animals, including neuroscience, vaccine development, and xenotransplantation, as well as demands within the scientific community to address a so-called shortage of NHPs through the creation of a "strategic monkey reserve," and for additional government funding for breeding facilities.[17]

In the United States, the NIH has signaled that they aim to increase the use of NHPs and recently asked the National Academies of Sciences, Engineering, and Medicine (NASEM) to "examine the current role of and future needs for nonhuman primates in biomedical research."[18] The NASEM committee's remit was to examine not *if* NHPs should be used, but *how*.[19] Their report affirmed the preordained conclusion that NHPs are necessary and will continue to be necessary for research to "advance scientific knowledge and protect human health," and that the need is "likely to grow." The report notes the perceived supply problem: "Ensuring a supply of NHPs that can meet the needs of the nation's biomedical research enterprise will require a commitment to supplying NIH-supported investigators from domestic resources. The development and implementation of a national plan for NHP research resources would help ensure the availability of NHPs to meet the nation's public health needs."[20]

Unlike most animals used in research, NHPs continue to be captured in the wild. The capture of free-living NHPs has negative effects not only on the individuals who are captured, but also on other free-living individuals of the same species, through the separation of families, disruption of social groups, and the reduction of populations that are already under threat from climate change, habitat loss, poaching, and human encroachment (see Section 1.3). Two species of macaques that are commonly used in research, pig-tailed and long-tailed macaques, are currently endangered in the wild, and capture for research use is a known contributing factor. Indeed, the NASEM report, citing Robitzski,[21] specifically acknowledges the role of capture-for-research as a threat to long-tailed and pig-tailed macaques, but frames this not as a problem for the macaques, but rather for researchers:

> The [International Union for Conservation of Nature, IUCN] has classified use in laboratory research as one of the primary threats facing macaques, and investigators are concerned about how this classification will impact biomedical research, a concern that further highlights the need for expanded

domestic breeding capacity. Although this classification does not have imme-diate consequences for ongoing primate research, it could potentially impact future research. The IUCN's decision could sway other influential institu-tions, such as [the Convention on International Trade in Endangered Species of Wild Fauna and Flora] or the U.S. Fish and Wildlife Service, to take similar action, which would have a much greater impact on investigators conducting research with these animals in the United States.[22]

Long-tailed and pig-tailed macaques are under extreme threat, and have been red-listed by the IUCN, "putting them three steps away from the final stage of the organization's seven-step scale, 'extinct.'"[23]

The IUCN estimates that, if things continue as they are now, both species are expected to suffer catastrophic population losses in the coming decades. The organization calculates that approximately 40 percent of the wild long-tailed macaque population has vanished in the last three generations (about 42 years) and over 50 percent of the pig-tailed macaque population has vanished in the last three generations (about 33 years).[24]

Rather than confront the devastating impact of the global wildlife trade in macaques destined for research laboratories through scientific innovation and actions that might reduce that impact everywhere, including accelerating the development of nonanimal methods, NASEM and the NIH raise the specter of the US Fish and Wildlife Service listing long-tailed and pig-tailed macaques as endangered. That agency's listing of chimpanzees as endangered pushed the NIH to stop funding research with chimpanzees in 2015 (see Section 3.4). Both entities have chosen to emphasize local workarounds, like increasing US breeding capacity, that perpetuate exploitation, captivity, and death for tens of thousands of monkeys every year and further incentivize the overreliance on NHPs in research (see Section 5.1).

For all of these reasons, there is now an urgent need to address the use of NHPs in research. Research with NHPs is subject to regulatory oversight motivated by welfare concerns. That oversight is much less strict than the constraints on human research, despite the well-understood similarities between humans and NHPs that are frequently used to scientifically justify using NHPs. Among the things humans and many NHPs (and a number of other nonhuman animals) have in common are their rich mental lives, their strong family and social bonds, and their lengthy period of adolescence and development. Many NHPs also have complex societies. Numerous harmful practices that are prohibited in research using human subjects are permitted in research on NHPs (and other sentient animals). For example, researchers are permitted to genetically modify NHPs (which can include the introduction of genetic mater-ial from humans and other animal species); intentionally induce illness or dysfunctions; inflict significant emotional and psychological distress; cause physical and permanent injuries (including amputations, spinal cord injuries that cause paralysis, the removal of eyes, and the implantation of screws, bolts, and electrodes); kill NHPs in order to study their tissues and organs; and kill them for a variety of other reasons, including colony population management.[25] Additionally, NHPs are subjected to forced breeding that includes artificial insemination, cloning, and the separation of infants from their mothers. Of all the animals used in laboratory research, NHPs are among those that live the longest, so their captivity and use in experimentation can go on for decades.

Nonhuman primates captured in the wild are subjected to the pain and terror of capture and transport, and separation from their families and social groups (see Section 1.3). Captive NHPs are subjected to the numerous harms of captivity, including the loss of freedom and autonomy, isolation from family, friends, and other members of their species, and unsuitable enclosures that do not meet their basic physical and psychological needs or permit them to express the full range of their natural behaviors, as well as ongoing fear, pain, and distress (see Sections 2.6 and 2.7).[26] Captive NHPs are harmed by captivity in many ways that are relevantly similar to the ways that humans are harmed by captivity and imprisonment.

Here, we describe a path forward and away from the use of NHPs in harmful scientific and research use. We argue for the moral necessity of harmonizing human and NHP research ethics, regulations, and guidelines in a way that *protects all primates*, human and nonhuman (recognizing that much of what we say also logically extends across animal scientific use). We call for the replacement of NHPs in research with human-relevant methods that do not merely shift research onto other sentient nonhuman animals. And we challenge publics, governments, and scientific communities worldwide to implement justice in the selection and use of all scientific subjects, including NHPs.

1.3 Spotlight: The Impact of Capturing Nonhuman Primates on Wild Populations

In early 2022, a truck crashed on a Pennsylvania highway, spilling its cargo across the road in freezing temperatures on a wintry day. The contents were 100 monkeys in crates bound for a laboratory in Florida. The crates were strewn and tumbled across the road, and some broke open. Four monkeys escaped. They were later captured and killed. Those 100 monkeys began their lives as free-living macaques. They had been captured in Mauritius, one of the largest exporters of monkeys for biomedical research. They endured a long, harrowing journey, flown to New York, loaded onto a truck, and then thrown across a highway. The survivors' journey ended in Florida, where it is likely that their lives will one day end, never escaping laboratory captivity.[27]

Most animals used in research are born in breeding or research facilities.[28] Nonhuman primates are an exception, and while many are bred in research facilities, they also continue to be captured in the wild.[29] In addition to the terror experienced by captured individuals, the trapping and export of NHPs for research purposes can impact the conservation of wild populations, and cause stress and suffering to wild monkeys.

The United States is one of the world's largest importers of live mammals, importing 63,672 mammals between 2012 and 2016, or 62.4 percent of the global mammal trade between 2012 and 2016.[30] During this time period, NHPs were the most traded mammals globally, amounting to 159,549 individuals and 94.8 percent of the legal global trade. The majority of legally traded NHPs are macaques.[31]

The IUCN's recent reclassification of long-tailed macaques as "endangered" is an example of how the biomedical industry can affect primate conservation. This species is a generalist, meaning they can live in a wide variety of environments. They live across Southeast Asia, yet their numbers in the wild have rapidly dropped by 40 percent in the last four decades.[32] The IUCN estimates that, as of 2023, long-tailed macaques number about 1,200,000 in the wild, with the population expected to decrease by 40–50 percent in the next forty years.[33] Macaques are the most traded primate species for research,[34] and the demand for long-tailed macaques increased during the COVID-19 pandemic as they are considered the main model for COVID-19 vaccine testing. Between 2008 and 2019, 450,000 live monkeys were sold for research. Of those, at least 50,000 were wild caught.[35] The United States is the primary buyer and importer of this species for research, and imported 30,000 in 2021 alone.[36] Tens of thousands of long-tailed macaques are bred for export in Southeast Asia, with Cambodia now the leading exporter; in 2020, 29,466 were exported from this country.[37] An unknown but likely large number of wild individuals are captured, sold to breeders, and then illegally exported as captive bred. Warne et al. found that the number of long-tailed macaques exported from Cambodia is larger than the number of macaques that could possibly be bred in Cambodian facilities.[38] The high demand and market for these monkeys incentivizes their wild capture. The trade in long-tailed macaques from 2010–2019 was worth 1.25 billion USD.[39] The US Department of Health and Human Services and Department of Defense combined have spent tens of millions of dollars on long-tailed macaques since 2019.[40] Pig-tailed macaques, another heavily used research species, have followed a similar trajectory and were also uplisted to Endangered on the IUCN Red List of Threatened Species. But the listing will not provide these species with protection in the United States. They must be listed under the Endangered Species Act and only then would federal regulations protect them and potentially impact their use in biomedical research.

Corruption and illegal activity complicate this issue. In November 2022 the US Department of Justice arrested eight individuals for their involvement in a monkey smuggling operation. Among those charged were Cambodian government wildlife officials and top executives at a breeding facility. In this scheme, wild long-tailed macaques were captured in Cambodia to supplement the supply from breeding facilities. Demand had exceeded the number of captive-bred monkeys available. The smuggled monkeys were imported to the United States, destined for a Charles River Labs facility in Houston, Texas, with 1,000 of the macaques falsely labeled as captive bred. At the time of this writing, the fate of the illicitly trafficked juvenile macaques has yet to be determined.[41] This is not, however, an isolated incident.[42] The increased demand for these monkeys for research continues to fuel this illegal trade and ultimately places pressure on the species as a whole. Additionally, these wild monkeys carry zoonotic diseases which can pose a health risk to humans with whom they come into contact.[43]

Macaques are not the only monkeys impacted by trade. The capture of owl monkeys in the Amazon Basin for biomedical research significantly reduced their populations in the areas where they were trapped.[44] During one period of study, researchers found that while permits allowed for the trapping of 800 individuals, 913 were in fact trapped due to poor enforcement. The trapping methods also impacted over 65,000 trees in the area.

The case of the Amazon Basin owl monkeys also shows how detrimental trapping can be to social units. Owl monkeys live in family units consisting of a monogamous father and mother with infant and juvenile siblings. Both parents participate in the care of infants.[45] Owl monkeys are a nocturnal species that sleeps in tree nests during the day. To capture the monkeys, groups of trappers place a net near the bottom of the nest tree during the day, clear all nearby vegetation that could provide escape routes, and then climb the tree and force the monkeys into the net at the bottom, capturing 1–3 individuals.[46] The bonded pair, or parents and their offspring, may be separated, which is psychologically catastrophic for the individuals involved.

Because group relationships are critical to security and well-being for many NHPs, the trapped monkeys likely experience significant fear. The family members left behind likely also suffer from the loss. Depending upon the trapped monkey's status in the group, there is potential for social upheaval within the group. Trappers sometimes prey on the same populations again and again; thus this repeated loss for local populations is likely to cause a significant degree of instability (with negative welfare impacts), loss of breeding members, and lower birth rates.

The process of trapping NHPs uses cruel and inhumane procedures and is highly stressful.[47] For example, monkeys typically live in social groups of kin and/or familiar individuals. Captured monkeys may be placed with unfamiliar monkeys, which can result in stress and aggression. They may be handled by untrained humans. They endure periods of quarantine, and are often housed in isolation. Transportation, both internationally and domestically, also has negative impacts on monkeys:

> The typical transport event for a research NHP approximates the following pattern. Shortly before shipment, animals are removed from their social groups (usually breeding groups) and placed in more typical laboratory housing (single caging or perhaps pair caging) for a period of pre-shipment monitoring and conditioning. Following this period of pre-shipping conditioning, the primates are normally transported singly in small cages. Transport is logistically complex, and the animals may travel and/or wait for many hours under varying climatic conditions. When the NHPs finally arrive at the destination facility in a new country, they are again quarantined – often in single cages. Long distance transportation across multiple climate and time zones is likely to induce substantial stress in the transported animals.[48]

In the United States, transportation regulations require food to be offered once every twenty-four hours and water every twelve hours for NHPs over one year of age. Individuals must be singly placed in transport cages with exceptions for mothers with nursing infants, male–female pairs, family groups, or pairs of juveniles. Transport cages must be large enough so the individual can turn around normally.[49] The stress and detrimental impact of transportation on animal welfare is so widely recognized that most major US airlines (including cargo shippers Federal Express and United Parcel Service) and many large international airlines no longer transport monkeys.[50] Within the United States and Europe, monkeys are transported by truck between breeding centers and laboratories. Many trucks are not climate controlled. Both air and truck transportation are associated with negative behavioral changes such as increased aggression and self-harm.[51] Transportation is also associated with physiological indicators of stress including increases in cortisol levels, decreased fertility, and changes in immune response. Transportation is thus another avenue for stress and poor welfare in addition to the ongoing stressors of captivity, daily laboratory life, and experimental protocols.[52]

In March 2022, the International Primatological Society issued a statement calling for biomedical research facilities to end their use of wild-caught NHPs, as well as those captured for biological sample collection (e.g., blood, tissue, etc.), when this requires the extended or permanent removal of individuals from their populations.

1.4 Protecting All Primates

At its best, ethics pushes us beyond our "personal horizon," beyond the immediate relationships we have with others, to give due consideration to the interests, needs, and vulnerabilities of those who are different from us.[53] When we refer to *morality* and *ethics* here we are not referring to different things. These two words are drawn from two languages – classical Latin and Greek, respectively – and mean the same thing in those languages. A common distinction is made between what people, communities, or societies tend to believe about ethics (or about our obligations to ourselves and to each other) and ethics as a reflective pursuit (where moral principles, decisions, or judgments are examined and tested for consistency with important values and principles). In our view, ethics as a reflective pursuit provides a guide to considering our moral obligations to others in a way that is principled and consistent and responsive to facts about the entities – the others – under consideration. Moral theories, like care ethics, deontology, Utilitarianism, or virtue theory attempt, in one way or another, to systematically order or explain the duties or obligations that survive reflective scrutiny (and sometimes provide tools for making future decisions). We do not here favor or endorse a particular moral theory or approach, but we reject arbitrarily favoring some individuals over others, or some species over others, when deciding how they should be treated or the protections they should enjoy.

A core commitment of ethics is formal justice, the idea that "like should be treated alike" or that "equals should be treated equally."[54] If it is ethical to treat two individuals differently, there must be some important and relevant difference that warrants that different treatment. To matter morally, their differences must relate to ethically important and relevant features of these individuals, whether it is their differing psychological capacities, interests, vulnerability to particular harms, or their significant social relationships. For example, we don't typically think that goldfish and hamsters should be treated exactly alike. They live in different environments, eat different foods, and have different social needs – goldfish are schooling fish, while hamsters are solitary and territorial mammals. Yet it would be morally wrong, and cause harm to both hamsters and goldfish to deprive them of food, or cause them injury, just as it would be wrong to do those things to a human in our care. What matters morally is that the individual is treated with equal consideration for their needs, desires, and well-being. Membership in a species, physical features (such as fur, scales, feathers, fingers, tails), and being cute or likable to humans are not typically relevant, except to the extent that they tell us something about the needs and vulnerabilities of the creature we are considering. When two individuals, regardless of their species membership, are not different in ways that matter morally, it is unethical to treat them with different regard for their well-being. That is what it means to treat equals equally, to say "like should be treated alike."[55]

Nonhuman primates often invoke strong protective responses in discussions of their use in scientific activities. This is easy to understand. Nonhuman primates bear a striking resemblance to humans both in their basic body and facial features and, more importantly, in their behaviors, relationships, and emotions. These similarities make it easier to relate to them, and to connect them to the kinds of ethical commitments commonly associated with humans, especially when we consider harms to NHPs.[56] Various capacities and traits that NHPs share with humans are often considered to be morally significant. Among these are their sentience (the capacity for conscious mental states like pain, pleasure, and a variety of emotions), their mental and intellectual abilities (including learning, tool use, problem-solving, and communication), and their social capacities. These traits shape the lives and experiences of NHPs, and also shape their welfare interests and vulnerabilities to harm.[57] For example, monkeys and apes live in a variety of social communities that are particular to their species. These social groupings include groups with multiple males and females, groups with a single male and multiple females, groups with a single female and multiple males, bonded pairs, and fission–fusion groups (which are fluid subgroupings within the community). There are also solitary NHPs. Many individual NHPs have unique and complex social networks, and develop life-long emotional bonds with siblings, cousins, and other relatives, as well as non-kin. The period of infant and adolescent development and dependency is particularly long in NHPs (as it is in humans), and it is the "primal" familial attachment relationship that sets the tone for future social interactions. Social learning, the process of learning from others, has been observed and studied in a number of NHPs and is vital to their healthy development. Social life is a prominent feature of the entire order of primates (as it is for many other animals as well).

Empathy is one capacity that is important for social agency and moral sensitivity in humans.[58] Monkeys and apes, as well as other vertebrate species (for example, rats and dogs), demonstrate this capacity in helping others, relieving another's pain, consoling others, or solving social problems.[59] Many NHPs can keep track of their own and others' social and normative interactions, suggesting they have a sense of fairness, or at least sensitivity to unequal treatment.[60] Fundamentally, these psychological capacities are evidence that they are aware of, and intentionally participate in, the lives of others. Unsurprisingly, evidence suggests there is a neural basis for this capacity: neuronal networks and brain regions associated with empathy-related behaviors in all primates (see Section 2.7).[61]

Our understanding of NHPs continues to deepen as the sciences advance. It is important, as more and more attention turns to our duties to NHPs (and to other sentient animals), to acknowledge their morally relevant similarities to humans whose moral importance is not questioned. Regardless of the nonhuman animals under discussion, our ethics should be principled rather than arbitrary and anthropocentric, which forces us to move beyond simply regarding humans as morally superior and more important than nonhuman animals. There is no doubt that NHPs are sentient, express an intelligence consistent with the physical and social worlds they must navigate in their lifetimes, and are vulnerable to physical and psychological harms that bear striking similarities to the human vulnerabilities that ideally guide our conduct toward each other.[62] In fact, the potential for psychological disturbance, distress, and suffering in NHPs is frequently exploited in psychological research – by causing NHPs to experience fear, loneliness, boredom, maternal–infant separation, and other trauma – to purportedly study psychopathologies that affect humans.[63] The harms NHPs experience in research are relevantly similar to the harms humans would experience under the same circumstances – and those common vulnerabilities are explained by shared capacities and traits. If human vulnerabilities help explain and motivate our moral duties to humans, then they should also help explain and motivate our moral duties to NHPs. What we do to NHPs in science matters morally.

In addition to psychological and social similarities, the genetic and physiological similarities between humans and NHPs have been exploited for scientific research and, considered together, are the basis of the purported scientific justification for using NHPs in place of humans (see Sections 1.5 and 5.1). At the same time, the *morally* relevant similarities, and in particular those that make NHPs and humans vulnerable to the same kinds of harms, are often disregarded within science, and not considered as reasons to restrict the use of NHPs (including outright bans for certain uses). This is arbitrary, as well as moral and scientific hypocrisy. The vulnerabilities of humans inspired the constraints, captured as principles – such as the *Belmont* principles – that inform human research ethics and guidelines.[64] These principles are reasonably extended to, and can be adapted for, ethical research with NHPs.[65] A commitment to just, ethical research requires such an extension.

It would be a mistake to think that only NHPs have capacities and vulnerabilities similar to those of humans, or that those animals with different capacities differ in ways that affect whether they matter morally. Nonhuman primates receive greater attention in discussions of our moral duties to them because it is simply easier to see in NHPs the cognitive, affective, and social capacities that matter morally to humans. But again, being entitled to moral treatment is not limited to primates, as anyone who shares their home with a dog, cat, hamster, bird, or goldfish can see. Drawing attention to our moral duties to NHPs should similarly call attention to the nearsightedness of any moral discussion that cannot extend to other nonhuman animals as well.

1.5 Spotlight: Harlow's Experiments with Infant Monkeys

Harry Harlow's experiments with infant monkeys are considered by some to be hugely important to behavioral science, revolutionizing the understanding of the role of social relationships in early development.[66] Others have condemned his work as unnecessarily cruel and inhumane. The kind of research Harlow pioneered is still being done today.

In the 1960s and 1970s, Harlow, a psychologist working at the University of Wisconsin, studied maternal deprivation in rhesus macaques. At the time, isolation experiments were common. The rationale was that these experiments could separate the contributions of nature and nurture. In order to study the effects of child separation on attachment and development, Harlow took newborn rhesus macaques from their mothers at birth and kept them in isolation from other monkeys. Some infants were completely isolated in a device that Harlow and his research assistant Stephen Suomi called the "pit of despair."

In social isolation, the infants exhibited disturbed behavior, staring blankly, circling their cages, and engaging in self-mutilation. Even without complete isolation, the infant monkeys raised without mothers developed social deficits. When the isolated infants were reintroduced to other monkeys, many stayed away from the others, and some died after refusing to eat. When female monkeys subjected to maternal deprivation later had babies of their own, some bit off the fingers and crushed the heads of their infants. The deprived monkeys showed signs of enduring psychological injury as adults.

Harlow devised an experiment in which he took infant monkeys from their mothers and gave them two inanimate "surrogate mothers": One was constructed of wire and the other was covered in soft terry cloth. Harlow found that even when the wire "mother" had a milk bottle and the cloth "mother" did not, the infant monkeys spent more time with the soft cloth "mother." He also demonstrated that the infants sought comfort from their surrogate "mothers" when faced with new and scary situations. Harlow's experiments have been credited with providing evidence of the importance of parent–child attachments and maternal touch in infant development.

Today, the University of Wisconsin is home to about 2,000 research monkeys at the Wisconsin National Primate Research Center (funded by the NIH) and the Harlow Center for Biological Psychology. Work inspired by Harlow's maternal deprivation studies continues there. In 2014, psychiatrist Ned Kalin planned experiments on the neurobiology of depression and anxiety that would separate newborn monkeys from their mothers at birth, using the same techniques as Harlow's. The infants were to be subjected to experiences – like seeing a live snake – intended to provoke fear and anxiety. After one year they would be killed and their brains analyzed.[67] The controversial experiments were opposed by some members of the Institutional Animal Care and Use Committee (the university committee charged with approving animal research). After public outcry and an online petition signed by over 300,000 people, the university announced that it was changing the study design, and would no longer separate infants and mothers. It is important to note that, in recent years, the Wisconsin National Primate Research Center has been frequently cited for poor care and violations of animal welfare that resulted in deaths and injuries – including amputations – of the monkeys housed there.[68]

Stephen Suomi, Harlow's protégé, also continued his work with infant monkeys while director of the Laboratory of Comparative Ethology at the National Institute of Child Health and Human Development, an NIH facility. Suomi's work, like Harlow's, forcibly removes newborn infant rhesus macaques from their mothers. For decades, Suomi studied how maternal deprivation affects biological processes such as brain activity and gene expression, and behaviors including alcohol consumption in the infants.[69] Actions by animal rights activists brought Suomi's experiments to the attention of four members of Congress in December 2014; they demanded an investigation by the NIH.[70] Within a year, the NIH had begun phasing out the controversial experiments and shutting down Suomi's lab.[71]

In late 2022, a paper published by Harvard neurobiologist Margaret Livingstone, evocatively titled "Triggers for Mother Love," inadvertently revealed cruel experiments being performed on infant monkeys. The paper described how macaque mothers could bond with stuffed toy monkeys after their infants were taken from them. It did not, however, describe why the infants were forcibly removed from their mothers shortly after birth: to be used in experiments on vision and brain development that included sewing shut the eyes of the infant monkeys. A storm of protest followed the publication of Livingstone's paper, with hundreds of scientists petitioning the journal, the *Proceedings of the National Academy of Sciences*, to retract it.[72]

The continuation of research like Harlow's decade after decade is an example of "technological lock-in," when scientists continue the work of their mentors, use established methods and technologies, and become entrenched in particular ways of studying problems, even when newer, better, more innovative methods exist.[73] Institutional pressures and financial self-interest also play a role, as it is easier for researchers to get money to continue a research program than it is to do work that is new and different. Animal research is increasingly, and rightly, under public scrutiny, and this can also increase entrenchment and lock-in, as researchers feel they must defend their work against critics. Lock-in is likely one of the reasons so few scientists are working on developing nonanimal research methods.

1.6 The Three Pillars of Ethical Research with Nonhuman Primates: Harmonization, Replacement, Justice

At present, harmful research with NHPs must comply with the regulatory schemes and guidance of the countries in which it takes place. Nowhere is this good enough, and conducting NHP research in a truly ethical way that acknowledges their moral importance requires the satisfaction of more rigorous guidelines and regulations modeled on those that apply to human subjects. No sustained and organized effort, comparable to the efforts that resulted in human research regulations and guidelines, has addressed the use of NHPs in research (nor the use of any other sentient animals except, perhaps, chimpanzees).[74] The use of NHPs has been addressed at various times in a piecemeal fashion, but whereas the starting presumption of human research guidelines is that humans have rights, including rights that cannot justifiably be violated, that has never been the initial presumption of examinations of NHP research (including that involving chimpanzees).[75] The predictable result is that even those documents that take an evidence-based, critical view of NHP research do not rule out research on rights-based or even welfare-based grounds, but rather by considering matters of scientific need or benefit for humans. Nor has any document approximated the scope or influence of *The Belmont Report*, the *Nuremberg Code*, or other foundational documents that lay out principles for ethical research with humans. Thus, even when NHP experimentation has been critically examined, it has been through an anthropocentric lens that unjustly magnifies human interests while minimizing or ignoring human obligations to other animals.

Here, we describe Three Pillars of ethical research and science with nonhuman primates: harmonization, replacement, and justice. *Harmonization* recognizes the moral similarity between humans and NHPs, and correspondingly, the need for guidelines and regulations for the scientific use of NHPs that are modeled on (and align with) those that govern research with human subjects. *Replacement* builds on the widely endorsed, even if ethically inadequate, "Three Rs" for humane research with animals explicated by Russell and Burch: Replacement, Reduction, and Refinement.[76] Replacement, put simply, requires replacing sentient creatures with nonsentient alternatives. While Replacement was given pride of place as the most important of the Three Rs by Russell and Burch, it has received the least priority in scientific practice, and in fact, today, far more animals – including far more NHPs – are used in research than were used in the 1950s. The increased scale and scope of NHP use in science is not compatible with replacement as we understand and interpret it. Finally, we build on the concept of *justice* as first described in *The Belmont Report* (1979), a grounding work on the ethics of research with human subjects that sets requirements of justice that include both scientific and ethical justification, with particular emphasis on safeguarding against the exploitation of vulnerable and captive populations in research. We interpret this to include NHPs. These Three Pillars support an ethical structure where no single pillar stands alone. Satisfying all three is necessary, for what might appear to be permitted by one pillar will be ruled out by another.

2 Harmonization

2.1 What Is Harmonization?

The first pillar of ethical research with NHPs is *harmonization*, or alignment of the ethics and regulatory schemes that guide science using NHPs and human subjects. The fundamental justification for harmonization is that NHPs are similar to humans in ways that are both scientifically and morally relevant. Moreover, that NHPs are used as substitutes for humans, often as a last step before first-in-human studies, suggests that the relevant scientific community believes they are relevantly scientifically similar. Where this similarity concerns our respective nervous systems and concomitant behavioral responses, we arrive at the capacities, traits, or characteristics used to defend human moral standing. We argue that they are no less relevant to the moral standing of NHPs. Thus, putting humans in one category of protections and NHPs in another is morally arbitrary, a matter of convenience, justified solely by anthropocentrism, which fails to acknowledge that the same ethical considerations apply to both.

A morally important common feature shared by some humans and NHPs used in research is their vulnerability. Internationally, research guidelines are especially attentive to the protection of vulnerable subjects and populations, prompted by historical abuses and research atrocities that exploited institutionalized children and the elderly, as well as enslaved, incarcerated, and captive persons (see Section 4.3). The Council for International Organizations of Medical Sciences defines vulnerable humans as those who are

> relatively or absolutely incapable of protecting their own interests. This may occur when persons have relative or absolute impairments in decisional capacity, education, resources, strength, or other attributes needed to protect their own interests. In other cases, persons can also be vulnerable because some feature of the circumstances (temporary or permanent) in which they live makes it less likely that others will be vigilant about, or sensitive to, their interests.[77]

The Belmont Report, which provides the ethical foundation for the US Common Rule, the federal law protecting human research subjects, notes the vulnerability of those who are institutionalized, dependent, and who cannot consent: "[They] may continually be sought as research subjects, owing to their ready availability in settings where research is conducted. Given their dependent status and their frequently compromised capacity for free consent, they should be protected against the danger of being involved in research solely for administrative convenience, or because they are easy to manipulate."[78]

The US Common Rule lays out special protections that restrict the use of incarcerated persons and children in particular, owing to their vulnerability to coercion and exploitation, and to their lack of or diminished ability to consent. These research restrictions on using incarcerated persons are informed by a history of past abuses, and similar constraints exist in international ethics guidance.[79] In Canada, the *Tri-Council Policy Statement* (TCPS 2) cites similar concerns about the vulnerability of incarcerated people and children.[80] The United Nations, in its Body of Principles for the Protection of All Persons under Any Form of Detention or Imprisonment (1988) states: "No detained or imprisoned person shall, even with his consent, be subjected to any medical or scientific experimentation which may be detrimental to his health."[81] The Council of Europe, Committee of Ministers declares that "Prisoners may not be submitted to any experiments which may result in physical or moral injury."[82] Although research with children is also more commonly restricted than research with adults, some policy documents recognize a child's agency in age/maturity appropriate ways. The TCPS 2, for example, recognizes the importance of respecting dissent, which can be expressed by very young children (perhaps even preverbal children) and precludes their participation.[83] All of these declarations and regulations recognize the unique vulnerability to coercion, exploitation, and force of those who are dependent or held captive or who have been historically oppressed.

The harmonization of human and NHP research ethics entails that NHPs must be treated as similarly "vulnerable subjects," like children, unable to consent to research, and also susceptible to coercion, exploitation, and overuse in non-beneficial and nontherapeutic research. Moreover, because much research on NHPs involves captive individuals and populations, harmonization entails treating captive NHPs like other institutionalized or incarcerated research subjects. Harmonization alone would not rule out all research or scientific activity on and with NHPs, just as human research guidelines do not completely rule out using children, or incarcerated and institutionalized persons. But it would provide additional protections and restrictions that are similar to those required for vulnerable humans, such as requirements that the research be relevant to and potentially beneficial to the population represented by the research subjects, and that the use of less vulnerable individuals, such as consenting adult humans, would not be scientifically sufficient. Importantly, harmonization would not involve more protection for NHPs than for similarly situated humans.

Restrictions that apply to research with all humans include: prohibitions on intentionally lethal research; the intentional infliction of serious injury, perman-ent disability, or other serious nonlethal harm (for example, nontherapeutic amputations or removals of organs and other body parts); forced breeding; nontherapeutic genetic modification; and the involuntary use of restraints. Moreover, human subjects cannot be held captive solely for purposes of scien-tific experimentation or study, nor can they be killed to harvest tissues and organs for future scientific use. Historically, ethical guidelines and regulations for human research specifically responded to practices such as these, which had previously been performed on captive populations including internees, prison-ers of war, institutionalized children, and incarcerated persons. In human research today, no study involving the intentional infliction of serious nonlethal harm, or the planned death of the subject, would be approved. Harmonization requires similar limits on NHP research. Significant, ethically motivated changes in science would be required in order to harmonize human and NHP research regulations and guidelines. There would be several practical implica-tions and requirements to ensure true harmonization that is responsive to ethics and science.

2.2 Ongoing and Retrospective Assessment of Research

There is ongoing scientific debate about the value of using NHPs to model humans in research.[84] The purported scientific justification for using NHPs in research is their similarity, and thus possible benefits, to humans. That justification is in need of thorough and continuous scientific evaluation that keeps pace with scientific developments, including the development of alternatives to using NHPs and other nonhuman animals. Whenever NHPs are used in research, a rigorous retrospective analysis of the concluded scientific project should be conducted by an unbiased third party. This type of analysis is described in European Union regulations on animal research.[85] Such an analysis should include consideration of whether the objectives of the project were achieved, and how and to what extent the research contributed to important and valuable societal benefits. Importantly, the analysis should also include an examination of the *actual* harms inflicted on the NHPs, the severity of the procedures used, and the number and manner of their deaths, keeping in mind that harmonization would prohibit intentional infliction of injury, disability, and death. In many jurisdictions, research with humans is subjected to ongoing safety monitoring and reporting to data safety monitoring boards and data monitoring committees to ensure that there is timely reporting and that subjects are protected from unexpected and serious adverse events and harms. This monitoring includes mechanisms for stopping research when it is clear that there are no significant benefits, or when the harms to subjects outweigh the expected benefits. The same monitoring, and the same limits, should exist for research with NHPs.

The addition of retrospective analyses of the kind we propose for NHP research are not currently required for research involving humans, and so this requirement appears to depart from the goal of harmonization. Firstly, we endorse requiring the same kind of analysis for research using human subjects. The safety of human subjects would be enhanced by this kind of retrospective analysis, and is consistent with the goal of *protecting all primates*. In particular, questions are frequently raised about the possible exploitation of research subjects in low-income and medically underresourced countries, where this kind of analysis would be especially valuable to ensure that the highest ethical and scientific standards are followed. Secondly, retrospective assessment would contribute valuable scientific knowledge about the scientific value and suitability of NHPs as proxies for humans in the research areas in which they are used for that purpose. As the suitability of humans in human-relevant research is not, in principle, in doubt, whereas the value and relevance to humans of research with NHPs remains open to question, the retrospective analysis is uniquely suited to help resolve this scientific question, and is both ethically and scientifically justified. It would contribute to the shared goal of ensuring that research with NHPs is in fact ethical, valuable, and beneficial.

2.3 Prohibition on Lethal Research and a Requirement to Provide Lifetime Care

There is increasing public concern about extremely harmful practices in science as well as a growing recognition that killing NHPs is inconsistent with treating them respectfully. The continuing momentum to curtail or ban the use of animals in cosmetics studies and testing offers a reminder of public concern for other animals in addition to NHPs. We call for a prohibition on lethal research, and on killing except where necessary to end otherwise unrelievable distress or suffering. This requirement would result in additional costs associated with appropriate lifetime care of captive NHPs. It would also appear to depart from current practices in human research, where the costs of lifetime care are not borne by scientists or scientific institutions. We identify this as another ethical gap in current human research requirements that should be addressed in cases where human research subjects suffer physical and psychological harms as a result of their participation in research.[86] Humans who voluntarily participate in biomedical research that benefits others should not be additionally burdened with the costs associated with injuries and other harms caused by that research. This is particularly important as biomedical research shifts to using subjects in low-income countries, where participants may lack access to the medical resources needed to treat research-related illnesses, injuries, or disabilities. The moral obligation to provide such care is incurred by the beneficiaries of the sacrifices made by human subjects, and the sponsors of research. Similarly, the moral obligation to provide lifetime care to NHPs used in science falls on the various beneficiaries – including societies that socially endorse or permit it and that benefit from it.

Nonhuman primate research and science, and the circumstances of captive, bred-for-research NHPs, are also uniquely different from research with humans. Captive NHPs used in science cannot simply be released to free-living environments, nor are they part of social groups that can care for them (as human children and institutionalized/incarcerated persons can be). Researchers, scientists, institutions, and NHP breeders are thus morally responsible for the lifetime care of NHPs who exist because of their actions. Moreover, ethical treatment requires that NHPs be housed in environments that can meet their physical, emotional, and social needs, and provide more than basic sustenance to keep them alive. This is too often not the case in standard laboratory housing. A 2016 survey of laboratories in the United States found 47 percent of monkeys were housed in "small enclosures intended for maintaining individuals housed singly or in small groups," often indoors.[87] Thus, nearly half are housed in socially deprived settings where their movements are restricted. In its study of biomedical research with chimpanzees, the Institute of Medicine concluded that chimpanzee subjects "must be maintained either in ethologically appropriate physical and social environments or in natural habitats" both during their use in research and afterwards.[88] We call for the same for all NHPs. Ethologically appropriate environments would be those that provide habitats that replicate important features of the natural environments in which free-living monkeys live, to ensure adequate and appropriate stimulation, activity, and opportunities for socializing and for exercising autonomy, as well as for engaging in species-typical behaviors like foraging and grooming. Scientists, as well as society at large, in whose name much scientific activity is conducted, incur an ethical debt to their subjects, whether they are humans or NHPs. They must, in the case of captive NHPs, assume the financial costs associated with ethically providing sufficient, humane, high-quality lifetime care in ethologically appropriate sanctuaries that can meet the social, psychological, and health needs of the species and of individuals (see Section 3.4).

Providing this kind of care would have significant practical implications, and the financial costs and availability of sanctuaries capable of providing high-quality lifetime care must be included in the calculus when the use of NHPs in research is contemplated and funded. At present, there are not enough sanctuaries to provide care even to the monkeys currently being used in research, who number in the tens of thousands in the United States alone. Thus, construction and maintenance costs for new sanctuaries must also be included in the calculus if science and research with NHPs are to continue. The current level of use is unsustainable. One sanctuary estimates the costs of caring for 15,000 monkeys – including construction and lifetime care for twenty years – at 562 million USD, or 37,466 USD per monkey. The costs of construction and care for the 1,000 long-tailed macaques at the center of a smuggling scandal will be 125 million USD.[89] If retired monkeys are simply replaced with other monkeys in research, the retirement system would become untenable and would perpetuate an eternal monkey mill of suffering. Retirement alone is thus not a permanent or viable solution.

2.4 Evaluating Necessity

Harmonization requires that the scientific use of NHPs must be strictly guided by both ethical principles and evidence-based scientific necessity. Like research with vulnerable humans, scientific use of NHPs must demonstrate that their use is necessary, that the risks are minimal, that all care is taken to minimize harms, and that there is no suitable substitute or alternative available. It is morally unjustifiable to use vulnerable humans or NHPs in potentially harmful research for which a suitable alternative is available; where scientific objectives can be achieved otherwise and with less risk of harm; in duplicative research, experimentation, or use; and in scientific activities that cannot be expected to achieve sufficiently important objectives and promote sufficiently large benefits; and where there is no demonstrable and important scientific necessity. As noted, retrospective analysis of all research and scientific use of NHPs is needed to obtain empirical evidence of the necessity of using them. The necessity of their use cannot simply be presumed, or accepted on the say-so of the scientists who do use them. The presumption that an instance of scientific use of NHPs is scientifically necessary or can achieve worthy, socially important goals must be questioned with the same rigor that is applied to research with vulnerable humans, and with an expectation of meticulous empirical and ethical justification.

When the Institute of Medicine Committee on Chimpanzees in Biomedical and Behavioral Research conducted its analysis of the necessity of using chimpanzee models, it concluded that "research use of animals so closely related to humans should not proceed unless it offers insights not possible with other models and unless it is of sufficient scientific or health value to offset moral costs."[90] Only two cases were found that met those criteria for biomedical research: studies of a limited number of monoclonal antibodies that were already in development at the time, and development of a hepatitis C vaccine (about which the Committee was divided concerning the need for chimpanzees). One consequence of the Committee's report, *Chimpanzees in Biomedical and Behavioral Research: Assessing the Necessity*, was that it and other contemporaneous developments, like the listing of chimpanzees as endangered by the US Fish and Wildlife Service, prompted the NIH to end its support for health-related research using chimpanzees. The Committee's work is a rare example of scientific research that questions the presumption of the scientific necessity of using an animal or species, and that also leads to a dramatic shift in scientific and funding priorities. We call for a similar analysis of the necessity and benefits of using other NHPs, with ongoing evaluation of new developments for as long as the scientific use of NHPs continues.

2.5 Global Alignment

Human research ethics are imperfect, and there is much room for improvement. Of particular concern is the practice of "ethics dumping," where restrictions on science in one country result in exporting scientific activity to countries with less strict human subject protections, effectively incentivizing a race to the bottom.[91] Ethics dumping is a serious human rights issue, and one that must be addressed internationally to bring human-based science regulations into global alignment. Similarly, if scientific standards are improved for NHPs in only one country, ethics dumping is likely to occur.[92] We urge a prohibition on ethics dumping in both human and NHP research, and a default to the highest and most protective standards of scientific use for both. Such a prohibition could be enacted through relevant revisions to international, national, and regional ethical codes and laws, and, importantly, through the organizations and agencies that currently fund international research. Better oversight and targeted punitive responses that focus on individuals, teams, and laboratories that fall short of or defy regulatory requirements can be expected to increase better compliance in some countries such as Canada and the United States. A commitment to international harmonization of standards for NHP research would be an important means of preventing ethics dumping and the exportation of scientific activities to countries with minimal or nonexistent regulatory standards. As data sharing is increasingly important, and cross-border data sharing is a stated goal of some large national and international research projects (such as the NIH BRAIN Initiative), useful disincentives to ethics dumping could include imposing restrictions on data sharing, and excluding violators from participating in international research projects, publishing in peer-reviewed scientific journals, and receiving grants and funding. There should be restrictions on commercial trade in NHPs with countries that do not meet accepted standards of ethical scientific conduct for NHPs.[93]

The application of human-similar ethical considerations to research with NHPs would result in significant limits on the scientific use of these animals. It would also represent an ethical alignment or harmonization that is justified by the welfare concerns already endorsed – in word if not in deed – by regulators, scientists, and various publics. It is justified by some of the same biological similarities that purportedly provide the scientific justification for using NHPs as substitutes for humans. It validates and gives ethical force to the scientific fact that nonhuman animals and humans are vulnerable to similar harms, a fact recognized in existing welfare guidelines. It acknowledges that what causes suffering in human subjects also causes suffering in NHPs who, like humans, are sentient and psychologically and often socially complex beings, for whom the potential for suffering is acute and of significant moral concern.

Harmonization would acknowledge and address the burdens and sacrifices to which NHPs have long been subjected for the protection of human research subjects, and the ethical obligations that follow from their involuntary sacrifices.

2.6 Spotlight: A Day in the Life of a Laboratory Monkey

Barbara J. King

Outside the medical laboratory, the day dawns with sunshine and a warm breeze. Monkey #1788 feels neither because his cage sits indoors, in a room with no windows. From his vantage point, the view, the artificial light, and the air remain identical from one day to the next.

The number 1788 comes from the tattoo this monkey had pressed into his flesh on the third day after his birth. That was nine years ago now.

Among the laboratory staff, the monkey is known informally as Chip. Alone in his cage, Chip is able to walk a few paces along the wire mesh floor and peer out at the other monkeys in their own cages. Sometimes, he is occupied for a few moments with his designated "enrichment" toy for that day, a cardboard tube, perhaps, or a bright red popsicle to eat. Mealtimes consist of Monkey Chow delivered through a chute and some fresh vegetables.

Chip is bored; he's been alone so long in this cage. For the first year of his life, he was kept in a bigger cage with three other young male monkeys. Being able to jump and play with them made him feel good. He drank milk from a bottle because he'd been taken away from his mother, but still, there was movement and life all around him. Now, Chip often slumps against the mesh and endures the passing time in that position, dozing on and off.

Sometimes, the monotony is broken. Two laboratory workers wearing masks and gloves approach Chip's cage. From many previous experiences over the years, Chip remembers what comes next. His bowels loosen and he snarls and jumps away but there is nowhere to go, and he is injected with anesthesia. As his legs become unsteady and his vision blurs, Chip is removed from the cage and carried on a mobile cart to a chilly room with bright lights overhead. When he wakes up again, he is back in his cage, still unsteady and with a new soreness in his head.

Chip pulls out some of his hair from his torso and legs, as he has done before and will do again.

Chip doesn't know the human name for his species, *Macaca mulatta* or rhesus macaque. He doesn't know that if he had been born in the wild he would have stayed with his mother and grandmother and aunts until, at puberty, he struck out and found a social group of his own where he would make a life among female mates and male allies and rivals. He doesn't know that there are tens of thousands of other monkeys, of his and other species, held in experimental laboratories all across the United States. He does know, as the day ends, that it's dark and he's alone.

2.7 Spotlight: The Neurological Effects of Captivity on Nonhuman Primates

Lori Marino

If there is one thing primates are best known for, it is their social lives. By nature, primates of many kinds live in groups of individuals made up of children, other family members, friends, and even competitors. But it all works because primate minds have evolved to live in complex communities where they are stimulated by different relationships and challenges. And because primate evolution, brains, and behavior have been shaped over tens of millions of years by their social lives they can only thrive in a natural social group.

While there are differences across primate species in terms of the specific ways they lead their lives, all primates need to care for their children, have the support of their family and friends, and have their minds kindled by the task of navigating through a complex social world. These social bonds are founded on emotions not unlike those of our own. We know this because not only are we so closely related to our NHP cousins that we share so much of our rich evolutionary history with them, but our brains are extremely similar.

Studies of primate brains show that human brains are not qualitatively different from the brains of other primates. Our brain is simply a larger version. And the parts of the brain that are involved in emotions, learning and memory, and responses to stress, are essentially the same. This system in the brain is called the limbic system and its structure and function have been highly conserved (unchanged) over evolutionary time. In fact, the limbic system of all mammals is fundamentally the same.

What does the limbic system do? Deep in the brain, the limbic system is a set of interrelated structures that are crucially involved in emotional responses (fear, sadness, etc.) and memories of events in our lives. It not only connects emotions with memories but it plays an important role in how the body responds to stressful situations.

When primates are held captive in labs the toll it takes on their brains is great. Nonhuman primates in biomedical labs are typically kept alone in small wire cages or enclosures (most without access to the outdoors) without any stimulation. The only time they experience social interaction is when lab staff seize them to conduct a procedure. Commonly, they are implanted with biomedical devices (e.g., brain electrodes), surgically impaired, or made ill. A few get to live in cages or enclosures with one or two other individuals, but these are not real social groups and this sometimes results in conflict.

We know from many studies across species that when primates and other mammals are forced to live in impoverished environments like those described here (i.e., those that do not provide enough social or environmental stimulation) many parts of the brain become damaged and stress hormones are released that harm the body and cause vulnerability to disease. The brains of individuals raised in impoverished environments, such as labs, show structural and chemical differences such as less branching on neurons, smaller capillaries, interneuron communication inefficiencies and lower brain weight, and reduced levels of serotonin.

The many monkeys used in the Harlow experiments (see Section 1.5) show the deleterious effects of these environments on the brains and behavior of young developing monkeys that result in a lifetime of abnormal and potentially self-injurious behaviors. For instance, captive primates and other animals engage in an abnormal behavior called stereotypies. These are repetitive behaviors that are indicators of chronic stress and harm to the brain systems connected to the limbic system. And there are many other abnormal behaviors that captive primates engage in, including self-harm (hitting one's head, self-biting, pulling one's hair out), anorexia, and behaviors indicative of depression – all of them signs of injury to important systems in the brain. These abnormalities are transmitted generationally as deprived babies grow up to be abusive or incompetent mothers. The brain impairments that result from being forced to live in a stressful, impoverished environment cause great suffering to these animals (as well as potentially compromised scientific findings). The harms to their brains can only be reversed by providing the kind of rich social life primates evolved to thrive in – environments that provide the stimulations their brains require to develop and flourish throughout their lifetime.[94]

3 Replacement

The second pillar of ethical research is *Replacement*, which calls for replacing NHPs with nonanimal alternatives in human-directed, harmful scientific use. Replacement is the first and foremost of the "Three Rs," the scheme for humane research with animals proposed by Russell and Burch in *The Principles of Humane Experimental Technique* (along with *Reduction*, or the use of the smallest number of animals consistent with good science, and *Refinement*, or the use of methods to reduce pain and distress and improve positive welfare).[95] The Three Rs are widely endorsed by scientists, regulatory agencies, and animal welfare agencies around the world.[96] However, to date, replacement has not been prioritized in the way Russell and Burch seemed to intend it, and as we understand it. While replacements for nonhuman animals were sparse and largely speculative when Russell and Burch proposed and prioritized them in

1959, today there are a number of human-relevant and human-biology-based technologies available and in development for biomedical research.[97] In some areas of research, human-relevant technologies have the potential to shift attention and resources away from the development of NHP "models" for humans, and toward the use of human-biology-based approaches to the study and promotion of human health.

Replacement of animals in science must remain sensitive to both scientific and ethical factors. Laws and regulations have sometimes hampered efforts to replace animals in science – for example, by requiring experimentation with animals prior to human experimentation – but, at their best, laws and regulations should also be informed by our best science and ethics. Better science, and more humane science, are goals shared by animal advocates and scientists who genuinely desire to improve human health. Despite their genetic and evolutionary proximity to humans, NHPs are not always the best models for humans in research.[98] Even chimpanzees, our closest evolutionary relatives, can fail to accurately predict how human beings will respond to pathogens and experimental substances like drugs.[99] Their unsuitability as proxies for humans has been repeatedly confirmed in numerous types of research. For example, the attempt to develop a chimpanzee model of AIDS in the 1980s failed when it was found that although chimpanzees could be infected with the HIV virus, almost none of them developed AIDS. The breeding of chimpanzees for that research contributed to the "surplus" seen today in the United States, particularly as killing "surplus" chimpanzees, unless it was welfare-indicated, was legally prohibited in the United States at the end of the twentieth century. As it stands, and to the best of our knowledge, chimpanzees have now been phased out in invasive scientific use worldwide (with the United States being the last country to end such use of chimpanzees). Many of the surviving chimpanzees "retired" by the NIH, including some still languishing in scientific facilities, are infected with HIV and other viruses (see Section 3.4).[100]

If we consider, in turn, some key scientific and ethical factors, we should first note that any effort to scientifically justify animal use must refer to the sought after scientific outcomes. So, when using animals as models, questions about their appropriateness must be asked and answered in ways that support their use before anyone can reasonably claim the beginnings of a scientific justification for animal use. We say "beginnings" because more needs to be addressed before an animal's use can be properly said to be scientifically justified. Issues such as design quality, sufficient statistical power, plans to report both negative and positive findings, and the competence of those doing the work must be factored into assessments of sufficient scientific justification as well. Two issues loom large here: The first is whether there is a history of success using the relevant animal as a model in pursuit of the proposed, sought after scientific outcome. The second is whether the experimental design sufficiently accommodates both the use history of the animals and their expected welfare during use.

The first issue connects, among other things, with ongoing issues of clinical and toxicological translation (see Section 3.1) when animals are used as models to acquire desired scientific outcomes. Where animals consistently fail to produce the sought after results, even where the scientific activities are of high quality, their continued use can no longer sensibly be said to be scientific-ally justified. Replacement is sometimes taken to imply that, in the absence of alternative methods, animal use can still be scientifically justified regardless of past failure – because the animals cannot be replaced. After all, doing *something* may look preferable to doing *nothing* if the stakes are high enough, even if that something has a very poor success rate. But consistent failure to produce sought after scientific results using animals, where the issue is not the quality of the science, still makes their use impermissible even in the absence of alternatives.

For those resistant to our analysis, much will turn on the moral status accorded to the animals who are to be used, and perhaps no definitive threshold of failure short of 100 percent will seem to support our claim. Significant translational failure may seem tolerable if the animals to be used are not as highly regarded morally as humans in research – and this value judgment is frequently implied by the claim that the scientific use of animals is the "ethical" alternative to using humans. But such use of animals is no longer being justified *scientifically* but, rather, *morally*. That value judgment requires justification, and as we have already argued, the justification is lacking.

The second issue connects with confounding factors that can emerge in contexts of animal use where the state of the animal introduces enough signifi-cant "noise" into the study as to undermine confidence in the epistemic value of the outcomes.[101] This kind of consideration can be found as far back as Russell and Burch's discussion of humane experimental technique,[102] and so does not require further exposition here. However, it is worth mentioning that this factor requires attention to individual animals that must constrain any attempted scientific justifications of animal use, and should caution against thinking that a successful scientific defense of any instance of animal use will stand as a universal scientific justification. Differences in welfare impacts among avail-able animals for scientific use may still preclude their use, even if some scientists, in some contexts, have available animals whose use satisfies other critical scientific considerations of the sort already suggested.

Evidence indicates that the use of NHPs and other living animals as human substitutes is frequently outdated and unproductive, conducted not because of genuine scientific necessity, but because of such factors as "lock-in" to traditional scientific practices, outdated regulations, and a lack of awareness of the availability of superior technologies.[103] Some regulatory agencies continue to require research on animals prior to regulatory approval,[104] and the availability of NHPs is supported by the existence of breeding and export programs around the world and, in the United States, by primate centers funded with taxpayer dollars by the NIH.[105]

Consistent with the goal of harmonization, we advocate the *complete replacement* of NHPs in harmful scientific activities, and nonminimal risk science that offers no direct benefit to the NHPs who are used. Mere reduction in the numbers of NHPs used, or the refinement of methods, husbandry, or housing, is not sufficient to make such scientific activities ethical or just. Importantly, a forward-looking and ethical approach will not engage in "species dumping" and simply use other animals in place of NHPs (see Section 3.3). Species dumping merely transfers harm, and when the animals are similar in morally relevant ways, it is no more ethical than the use of the NHPs themselves. Achieving this goal will require more concerted and meaningful investment in the science and research needed to develop and implement the adoption of human-relevant research methods. A significant portion of the funding for research and development comes from public monies distributed by governmental agencies – such as the NIH (which devotes a mere 0.003 percent of its research and development funding specifically to research on alternatives to animals)[106] – to promote science that is in the public interest. There is an immediate need for significantly increased funding for science training programs and research grants to study, develop, and implement human-relevant methods for investigating human health and disease that can replace the use of NHPs. This is both a scientific and an ethical imperative. As Johnson argues in a paper critiquing the NIH BRAIN Initiative's stated intention to continue using NHPs in neuroscientific research,[107] more than scientific lip service to replacement is needed: "If, as is widely acknowledged, NHPs are the animals of most ethical concern, then replacing NHPs with human-relevant alternatives should be a scientific priority of a neuroscience that aspires to be ethical, transparent, and beneficial, and aspires to honestly engage with the substantive, difficult, and unresolved ethical questions and concerns that arise in its practice."[108]

3.1 Translational Failure: Does Research with Nonhuman Primates Save Human Lives?

There's a saying in biomedical research: "Mice lie and monkeys exaggerate."[109] Scientists who experiment on animals know that the results of their research can be misleading, and often fail to translate into knowledge that advances human health. The problem is not only recognized by scientists; it has been studied extensively.[110]

Translation in the human-directed biomedical sciences is the process whereby observations made and data acquired in scientific studies are turned into interventions that improve the health of individuals and the public. In the realm of research conducted on NHPs and other animals, successful translation occurs when an intervention, whether it be a drug or a vaccine, a surgical device or a technique, a diagnostic method, or another innovation that has been tested in an animal proves to be broadly effective and safe for use in humans. The opposite of translation is attrition, or the failure of successful translation, which can occur at various stages in the development of new interventions. It is known that the clinical attrition rate of investigational drugs is roughly 90 percent, a result that Garner describes as "shockingly poor translation."[111] In other words, the vast majority of new drugs that are developed and tested using animals end up failing when they are tried in humans.[112] Those drugs appear to be safe and effective in animals, but turn out not to be safe or effective in humans. This "translational failure" not only causes harm to the millions of animals used in experiments, but it can also cause harm to humans when those drugs are tested on them. For example, a class of drugs that was proposed as a treatment for stroke, NMDA channel blockers, caused side effects such as nausea and hallucinations, as well as life-threatening side effects including low blood pressure and respiratory arrest when administered to humans.[113] None of those side effects were observed when the drugs were tested in animals.

Elias Zerhouni, former director of the NIH, a major funder of health-related research, once lamented the focus on animal models to study human health:

> We have moved away from studying human disease in humans. We all drank the Kool-Aid on that one, me included. With the ability to knock in or knock out any gene in a mouse – which "can't sue us" – researchers have over-relied on animal data. The problem is that it hasn't worked, and it's time we stopped dancing around the problem ... We need to refocus and adapt new methodologies for use in humans to understand disease biology in humans.[114]

Stroke research provides an excellent example of the failure of animal experimentation, where the failure rate is close to 100 percent. In stroke research, there's even a saying inspired by that failure: "Everything works in animals, but nothing works in people."[115] Stroke is a leading cause of death and disability in industrialized nations, so there is a great need for effective treatments. Since 1960, more than 1,000 drugs and therapies for stroke have been tested in thousands of experiments on animals.[116] Of these, 37 drugs have been tested in humans in 114 clinical trials. Only one effective drug has come out of those experiments: the clot-busting drug tissue plasminogen activator (tPA). Unfortunately, to be effective tPA must be administered within three or four hours of a stroke, which is not always possible with human stroke patients. The drug also increases the risk of dangerous bleeding in the brain,[117] so an effective therapeutic alternative is needed and this has been the subject of many animal studies.

Part of the reason for the failure of stroke research is that to study stroke treatments in animals, stroke-like conditions must be induced using methods that do not replicate the way strokes naturally occur in humans. Methods for inducing stroke-like brain injuries in animals include: clipping blood vessels or cuffing and cauterizing arteries; introducing chemical or mechanical "clots"; inducing cardiac arrest; and inducing asphyxia using neck cuffs and tourniquets, potassium cyanide, nitrogen, and carbon dioxide.[118] Surgeries, including craniotomy (opening the skull) or accessing blood vessels through the eye, sometimes removing the eye, are also used.

The failures in stroke research are so serious and so well recognized that stroke researchers have established a set of recommendations, known as the STAIR (Stroke Therapy Academic Industry Roundtable) guidelines, to improve stroke research. One of the recommendations is to use cats and NHPs because their brains are more like human brains. Researchers admit, however, that there is no evidence that using cats or NHPs would result in more successful research.[119] This is an example of scientists being committed to using animals, even when the evidence shows that using animals in stroke research has led to numerous failures in stroke research.[120]

Until recently, chimpanzees were used to study a number of human health disorders, in addition to their use in studies of language, movement, development, evolution, and even space flight. As the closest genetic and evolutionary relative of humans – with a genome estimated to be approximately 95–99 percent identical to that of a human – chimpanzees were considered the ideal animal model for research that could not be conducted on humans.[121] Bailey examined the use of chimpanzees in cancer research, and found that even among these close genetic relatives, genomic variations were significant enough to result in large differences in human cancers:

> A recent structural genomics study, which compared the regulation of apoptosis between humans and chimpanzees, acknowledged that nutritional and ecological differences contributed to changes in cancer incidence between the species, but could not "coherently explain" an order of magnitude increase in cancers of the breast, ovary, lung, stomach, colon and rectum in humans. Instead, the authors implicated some of the estimated 40 million differences (of various types) between the human and chimpanzee genomes, which determine susceptibility and tolerance – as seen in different human populations.[122]

Bailey has claimed that more than half of the published research papers reporting on scientific experiments with chimpanzees have never subsequently been cited. Less than 15 percent were cited in other papers relevant to human medicine, but "an in-depth analysis of these studies revealed that the chimpanzee experiments had contributed very little, if anything at all, to the outcome of those papers reporting an advance in human clinical practice."[123] Bailey interprets this as an indication of the relative lack of importance of biomedical research using chimpanzees for human health, and concludes that "chimpanzees simply cannot constitute a vital part of research into cancer, or indeed any other disease."[124]

> It would therefore seem that Russell & Burch's "high-fidelity" fallacy – the mistaken notion that the more a model superficially resembles the thing being modelled, the more suitable it is for elucidating the phenomenon in question – is highly applicable to cancer research in chimpanzees, and indeed to chimpanzee research on human diseases more generally. When our closest genetic relative has contributed so little to combating cancers that have cost hundreds of millions of lives and hundreds of billions of research dollars, it is unscientific to claim that they must remain a crucial and necessary tool in cancer research.[125]

Knight's study of citations similarly suggests that chimpanzee experiments have low utility, noting as well that only a subset of studies are even reported in the scientific literature, which may paint an even more unfavorable picture of the value of the scientific experiments performed on chimpanzees.[126]

> Given that research of lesser significance is not published at all, these published chimpanzee experiments can be assumed to be those with the greatest potential for advancing biomedical knowledge. Consequently, these results indicate that the majority of captive chimpanzee research generates data of questionable value, which makes little obvious contribution toward the advancement of biomedical knowledge.[127]
>
> However, it is reasonable to expect that if chimpanzee research had truly been of critical importance during struggles against major human diseases, as claimed by advocates, such chimpanzee studies would be cited by papers describing methods efficacious in combating those diseases. The only remaining possibility is that none of the struggles – to which chimpanzee research purportedly made major contributions – resulted in effective, published solutions.[128]

The number of times a scientific research paper is cited by other papers is frequently taken to be an indicator of its influence in its respective field – that is, citations are correlated with influence and indicate that a work is part of the scientific conversation and is shaping further research. There are confounding factors that might limit the inference that citations are evidence of influence, including citation practices within the relevant scientific community and what is required by journals or funding agencies. But the approach taken by Bailey and Knight, as we describe, at least poses a reasonable challenge to those who hold that preclinical research is relevant to first-in-human scientific studies. (We do not deny that confounding factors exist nor preclude the possibility that a reasonable rejoinder can be made, but a rejoinder is required.)

While chimpanzees are the species most closely related to humans, they have been largely "retired" from use in scientific experiments (and, to the best of our knowledge, wholly "retired" from invasive science), in part due to ethical concerns about these close cousins, and in part due to the high cost of keeping them. Yet, as Knight notes, this means more distantly related species, including other NHPs, are being used in their stead. He holds that it can be reasonably inferred that they are even less suitable as a "model" of humans and their disorders:

> it is highly likely that other species are even less efficacious when used as experimental models of humans in biomedical research and toxicity testing. Given the many millions of other species used annually for these purposes (particularly in the case of rodents); the profound ethical and financial costs incurred as a result; and the adverse consequences for human health – if other, potentially more efficacious research models are consequently deprived of funding – systematic reviews of the utility of other laboratory species in advancing human healthcare are also urgently warranted.[129]

Indeed, Bailey also argues that the evidence supporting the use of NHPs is thin, with what appear to be numerous notable failures of such research, including in toxicology research where NHPs overpredict the toxicity of cancer drugs and yield false positives compared to human results (in other words, the drugs are more toxic in NHPs than in humans). Results in developmental toxicity, which studies teratogens that can be harmful to fetal development, correlate with known human teratogens only 50 percent of the time.[130] Alzheimer's disease and stroke research, as well as Parkinson's disease research, have similarly failed to yield benefits for human health. Chimpanzee research on HIV/AIDS is a notable scientific failure (see Section 3.4) but the situation seems no better for other NHPs:

> In HIV/AIDS research, the use of macaques is widely considered to lead to failure and to be of questionable human relevance. Many, if not all, of some 100 different types of HIV vaccines were tested in monkeys with positive results, yet none provided protection or therapeutic benefit in humans, due to major differences in SIV-infected macaques compared to HIV-infected humans.[131]

To date, all HIV vaccines that have been trialed in humans have failed after similar vaccines targeting Simian Immunodeficiency Virus (SIV) and Simian–Human Immunodeficiency Virus (SHIV) infection appeared successful in NHP models.[132] The STEP trial, a clinical trial conducted in South Africa, used a vaccine based on one that showed minimal protection against SIV infection in macaques.[133] The experimental human vaccine, alarmingly, appeared to increase the rate of HIV infection in some individuals who received it, forcing the manufacturer to halt the trial.[134] The failure of NHP models in HIV vaccine research has thus contributed to the failure of the overall research program, which relies on NHPs, and has at times resulted in genuine harm to human research subjects. This situation echoes the experience of using NHPs in polio vaccine research more than seventy years ago, when failed attempts to produce vaccines using virus derived from monkeys killed some human research subjects (see Section 5.1). In addition to the NHPs who suffer grievously as research subjects, humans also suffer because of the scientific failure of NHPs as models of human systems and disorders.

Shanks and Greek summarize the *scientific* arguments against using NHPs in HIV research:

> HIV is a case in point; the use of nonhuman primates to predict the human response to HIV has been unsuccessful. Vaccines that have protected nonhuman primates from HIV did not protect humans, and the mechanism of HIV attack varies among primates. Humans and nonhuman primates do share characteristics important to drug and disease response, but these shared characteristics are not quantitatively or qualitatively adequate to allow prediction in the scientific sense of the word ... does the use of nonhuman primates achieve positive and negative predictive values sufficient to claim that they are predictive of human outcomes? The answer is that they do not.[135]

Reflecting on the use of NHPs in medical science, Bailey concludes that "there is a paucity of evidence to demonstrate the positive contribution or successful translation of NHP research to human medicine, that there is a great deal of often overlooked data showing NHP research to be irrelevant, unnecessary, even hazardous to human health and to have little or no predictive value or application to human medicine."[136]

As Pamies and Hartung observe, "There is no good science in bad models."[137] The failure of animal research to translate to effective treatments for humans has caused unnecessary animal suffering and death. Those failures, and an unjustified commitment to using animal models even when evidence points to their unsuitability, also hold back medical progress, resulting in suffering and death for humans as well.[138]

3.2 Incentivizing Change

We have outlined some of the consequences of taking seriously our highest ethical standards in the form of formal justice (that like should be treated alike) – for example, the prohibition of intentionally lethal research, and the provision of lifetime care after scientific use. Adding to those details here can show how a properly ethical science incentivizes change.

If we see an alignment of ethics standards across the domains of human-based and animal-based science, a prohibition of intentionally lethal research and the provision of lifetime care will place significant financial pressures on funding agencies and institutions that keep captive NHPs used in science, as we have already outlined. But this is not a burden that agencies and institutions should bear in isolation. We must not forget that animal use in liberal democracies occurs because of social license. That is, animal use in these societies is a privilege provided by laws, regulations, policies, and the concomitant funding infrastructures. This means that the financial burden we have outlined is one that should also be borne by the relevant societies that socially license and tacitly endorse the scientific use of NHPs.

This will have the add-on effect of making animal scientific activities much more expensive, an expense currently avoided through such immoral practices as killing NHPs who could otherwise live well in supportive and ethologically appropriate environments. As we mentioned above, they cannot simply be released into the wild, even if they were originally captured from the wild. Most animals are killed after scientific use regardless of their welfare status,[139] and this fails to acknowledge the debt incurred by our use of these animals for our own benefit.[140] Benefit in this instance should be interpreted quite broadly. As professionals, scientists are motivated to pursue their scientific work for reasons other than altruism, although we are not minimizing that motivation here. Those additional reasons include advancing their careers, enlarging their role in the scientific "conversations" of which they are a part and for which they trained, advancing knowledge, training and employing another generation of scientists and animal technicians, and supporting colleagues. These are not ignoble reasons, indeed many are laudable. Our purpose in highlighting them is to remind the reader that they are benefits that arise, among other things, from using nonhuman animals in scientific activities for which scientists receive institutional, financial, and even societal support. Importantly, such benefits arise from animal scientific use even when it is not human-directed, so this is a much broader sense of "benefit." These benefits are also advantageous to the societies in which these scientists work, and societies where other scientists use that work to further advance the relevant sciences.

Thought about in this way, it is reasonable to think that we all owe something to those animals used in science after that use comes to an end. We have benefited from their almost entirely involuntary use and in ways that can cost these animals dearly. To resist thinking that we owe them a debt cuts to the core of quite ordinary ways of thinking about debts incurred from beneficial sacrifice (e.g., wartime service). Understandably, we might balk at the idea of describing animal scientific use as "beneficial sacrifice" but "sacrifice" is a euphemism frequently used in scientific settings to refer to killing animals in the pursuit of sought after outcomes.[141] Taking that use of the term at face value quickly ties into our point here. A sense of incurred debt is what motivates the care we, as societies, owe our active and retired armed forces personnel and first responders. Arguably, this is both an expression of gratitude for actions done for our benefit and also a recognition that, but for their efforts, others, including ourselves, may have had to do it in their stead. It should be fairly apparent how this applies to the scientific use of NHPs and other animals. These animals are putatively used for our benefit and, but for that use, human members of our communities – if alternatives are unavailable and the need for scientific advances is pressing – would have to be used. That these animals are mostly used against their will should only increase that sense of indebtedness.

Thus, NHPs not only should be retired and rehomed where that is possible, but, in liberal democracies, the costs of such rehoming and care fall on all of us who have socially licensed their use. Avoiding that cost by killing those to whom we owe a debt is hardly ethical and should not be done in societies that aspire to be just. As any society's ability to pay this incurred debt is limited, and this is true even of high-income countries like the United States and Canada, this provides a significant incentive to develop and embrace nonanimal alternatives.

3.3 Ethics Dumping and Species Dumping

As we have already mentioned, ethics dumping refers to escaping ethical and regulatory constraints on an activity by relocating to a setting where those constraints are less restrictively applied or are altogether absent. In science, this can involve relocating scientific activities to less restrictive countries or jurisdictions in order to escape ethics constraints. This is a phenomenon in both animal-based and human-based science and it reminds us that the hard-won changes in ethics standards governing human-based science are by no means universally accepted by scientists, even to this day.[142]

An example of ethics dumping in scientific activities involving chimpanzees is captured by the fate of ex-biomedical research chimpanzees in Liberia. The chimpanzees in Liberia are the survivors of use in vaccine research sponsored by the New York Blood Center (NYBC) and performed at a research facility known as Vilab II between the mid 1970s and 2005. Rather than being killed when their scientific use ended, the chimpanzees were housed on islands in Liberia that lacked adequate food or water to nourish them. Until 2015, the NYBC employed caretakers to provide food and water for these chimpanzees and their offspring. When it decided to financially abandon the chimpanzees, the NYBC tried to deflect responsibility by highlighting that the chimpanzees were owned by the Liberian government and so were effectively their problem. Although the NYBC reached an agreement with the Humane Society of the United States to help provide funds to support the care of the chimpanzees in 2017, it has refused to take on sole responsibility and so its legacy of trying to deflect moral responsibilities continues. After all, these chimpanzees only exist in their current predicament because of the actions of the NYBC, whose deeds qualify as ethics dumping.

Another hint of ethics dumping is found in the Institute of Medicine chimpanzee report which claims that a number of investigators from countries "outside the United States have supported limited use of chimpanzees in the United States."[143] Alongside a claim that "[m]any countries have legislation banning the use of great apes, and therefore chimpanzees,"[144] the report implies that some scientists have been working around bans in their own countries. Expanding on this claim a little later, it suggests that a number of "non-US-based companies or . . . academic investigators" from Belgium, Denmark, France, Italy, Japan, and Spain have sponsored US-based biomedical research (e.g., on hepatitis C and vaccine research) using chimpanzees.[145] The relevant sponsorships, as described in the report, qualify as ethics dumping.

It should go without saying that where regulations or policies reflect sound values and commitments, ethics dumping is immoral. That is to say, where regulations or policies are supported by sound ethical reasoning, purposefully working around those regulations or policies for anything other than better ethical reasons (e.g., securing a greater good) is to act unethically. That chimpanzees should enjoy the kind of protections reflected in banning their use in significantly harmful scientific activities is well-supported by considerations of formal justice, given our best scientific knowledge of chimpanzee characteristics, capacities, and traits. It follows that if human-directed scientific activities cannot be ethically accomplished using humans they cannot be ethically accomplished using chimpanzees, and if they *can* be ethically accomplished using humans – given that humans are the best model for humans – they *should* use humans. Consequently, human-directed scientific activities that cause such harm to chimpanzees are immoral, and they were immoral when companies or investigators were sponsoring chimpanzee research in the United States. The

NYBC is an even clearer example of ethics dumping as it acquired a duty of care for the chimpanzees arising from their acquisition and use by scientists working for the organization and have refused to (fully) fulfill that duty, something that seems to have been made possible by inadequacies in Liberian law.

As noted earlier, species dumping occurs where some sentient nonhuman animals are used instead of others, despite their similar moral status. In animal scientific use this is compliant with the Three Rs as generally understood (the Three Rs are not concerned with moral status) and captured by the distinction between absolute and relative replacement. Absolute replacement is the replacement of sentient animals with insentient models or materials. Relative replacement is the replacement of some sentient animals with others who are thought to be "less sentient" or less vulnerable to the harms that the replaced animals would experience (e.g., sentient animals who are thought to be incapable of a certain degree of pain or suffering).[146] Relative replacement intersects with one of the two prominent "languages" of ethics. The "language" of permissibility and impermissibility allows us to talk of actions that do no wrong (these are permissible actions) and actions that do wrong (these are impermissible actions). But another common ethics "language" tracks a rather historically old distinction between lesser and greater evils. This allows us to talk about what is ethically better or worse, even where both options are impermissible, that is, even where the better option still involves doing wrong. After all, a lesser evil is still an evil.

Within our ethics framework, we reject the view that there are no other animals who share with humans relevantly similar characteristics, traits, or properties that support according them the moral significance we currently accord humans. A wrong in any animal-based science occurs when these nonhuman animals are denied the moral significance they are due. In our view, that routinely happens in cases of relative replacement. That is, animals who should enjoy equal moral significance are routinely used instead of other sentient animals who currently have greater protection or sympathy from those making decisions about use. Examples include using hamsters or ferrets instead of NHPs in virus research. Another example is the growing use of fishes in scientific research. Ironically, experimentation with fishes, who were once widely believed to be incapable of pain, led to scientific confirmation of their sentience, as well as a number of other "discoveries" about the capacities of fishes.[147] This is to be expected whenever relative replacement favors using some species or taxa over those known to be sentient and vulnerable to harm. Another example is the use of invertebrates, including octopuses and other cephalopods, instead of vertebrate animals.

A concerning form of species dumping that continues to garner attention is the creation and use of human–animal chimeric models. We have made much of the reported failures of animal models in translational science.[148] One supposed work-around is to genetically modify animals to "humanize" them, that is, modify them to express something like the human disorders or traits researchers aim to study. An example is the so-called autistic monkey.[149] "Humanize" is a deeply problematic term here, as these animals remain decidedly nonhuman, and so-called humanization implies the moral superiority of humans such that moral concern about "humanized" animals reflects a concern for "the human" or "proximately human."[150] The German Ethics Council, for example, noted concerns about human moral status being transferred to chimeric animals along with human genes.

> A particular ethical issue is whether the transfer of individual human genes might sometimes alter important characteristics of the receiving species in such a way as possibly to affect the animal's moral status. Drastic modifications of this kind are at least conceivable at [a] biological level.
>
> Particular ethical issues are raised by the possibility that the transplant of human nerve cells or their precursors into the brains of animals – in particular, primates – might give rise to human capabilities in the animal that could in certain circumstances alter its moral status.[151]

A standard presumption of those who argue against moral consideration for these human–nonhuman chimeras is that one need only demonstrate that the "humanized" monkey or mouse is not human *in the right way* to effectively exclude them from moral consideration.[152] Johnson has argued that this ignores the many relevant traits these animals already share with humans: "Traits commonly associated with moral status in humans, including psychological, emotional, and social complexity, culture and the use of language and tools, consciousness, intelligence, problem-solving, autonomy, moral agency, and even concepts of and rituals associated with death are found in numerous species."[153]

"Humanizing" animal models seemingly makes scientific sense. If it is true that genetic differences are responsible for animals being unsuitable models for humans – although this has not been conclusively established – then diminishing those differences should be a way to deal with the translation problem. In order to "humanize" an animal model, human cells must be inserted into the animal used as a model with the purpose of those cells proliferating and sufficiently integrating with the rest of the animal's body and biological functions. This permits study of the human cells and tissues in a whole, living system without violating prohibitions surrounding human use. As these cells and tissues are human (in some sense), the use of the relevant animal model would not, in theory, be prone to the kinds of failures mentioned earlier. Indeed, leading hypotheses regarding translational failure can be tested through the use of "humanized" animals.

The rise of genetically modified and "humanized" animal models introduces a pernicious element resistant to some of the aspirations mentioned in this Element. Some time ago, Rollin remarked on the refinement challenges presented by genetically modified animals, who are predisposed to mimic conditions or pathologies that will cause a great deal of stress and suffering. Standard refinement interventions are likely to be difficult or inadequate to relieve the suffering of these animals.[154] Retiring and rehoming animals who are, in a real sense, born to suffer, looks to be cruel rather than ethical or just. What is more, regulations or policies commonly ban the release of these animals, even if they could live out the remainder of their lives in a worthwhile way. This has been interpreted as a reason why they do not qualify for retirement and rehoming even if their welfare status favors it.

Regulations concerning these modified animals represent not so much a way around the Three Pillars framework as its contravention. To use them in human-directed science incurs the same societal debt as using nonmodified animals. If what we have done to them precludes their retirement and rehoming, our debt goes unpaid. A quick death is not repaying that debt; indeed, it is not an act of mercy where their poor welfare status is intentional. One cannot, without hypocrisy, intentionally bring about extreme pain or suffering and then call oneself merciful by killing the individual in that intentionally induced state of pain or suffering. Where we can anticipate that our societal debt must go unpaid, our framework requires that the relevant animals are never created in the first place.

3.4 Spotlight: The Alamogordo Chimpanzees – A Failure of Replacement and Humane Retirement

Replacement ranks first among the Three Rs – which are widely recognized around the globe as constraints on animal use in science. The Three Pillars asks for more: harmonization of animal and human research ethics, and justice in the selection and use of NHPs in research. The Three Pillars also requires that NHPs used in research should be released to suitable sanctuaries for the remainder of their lives. In 2015, the NIH retired all of its chimpanzees from research. The move was a partial success story, which followed years of failure by the NIH to replace chimpanzees in harmful research.

During the early days of the AIDS pandemic, chimpanzees were bred in large numbers for HIV/AIDS research. Chimpanzees are among the closest genetic and evolutionary nonhuman relatives to humans, but it turned out that although chimpanzees could be infected with HIV, the virus that causes AIDS in humans, they did not become sick as humans do. The failure of AIDS research with chimpanzees led to a "surplus" of chimpanzees.[155]

The NIH decision to stop funding invasive chimpanzee research resulted from three important developments. First, the US scientific organization, the Institute of Medicine, issued a report undermining scientific claims about the broad necessity of using chimpanzees in invasive research. Second, the NIH's own Council of Councils report supported phasing out most invasive research using chimpanzees;[156] and finally, the US Fish and Wildlife Service designated "captive chimpanzees as endangered."[157] These, combined with the "significantly reduced demand for chimpanzees in NIH-supported biomedical research," compelled then NIH Director Francis Collins to change course, and the decision was made to stop funding chimpanzee research, retire the existing "surplus" chimpanzees, and transfer them to sanctuary.[158]

In 2000, the Chimpanzee Health Improvement, Maintenance, and Protection Act (CHIMP Act) became law.[159] This federal law prohibits the "humane killing" of "surplus" chimpanzees except when it is in the individual's best medical interests; created a sanctuary system for former research chimpanzees; and requires that federal agencies that own chimpanzees

> provide for the lifetime care of chimpanzees that have been used, or
> were bred or purchased for use, in research conducted or supported by
> the National Institutes of Health, the Food and Drug Administration, or
> other agencies of the Federal Government, and with respect to which it
> has been determined ... that the chimpanzees are not needed for such
> research.[160]

In deciding to retire all of its chimpanzees, the NIH did not release all of them to sanctuary, which is in violation of the letter and spirit of the CHIMP Act.[161] Dozens of chimpanzees remain at the Alamogordo Primate Facility in New Mexico, confined in the same laboratory where they were once experimented upon and traumatized. They live in cages, and only have access to the outdoors from within covered wire enclosures. The reason given for not releasing these chimpanzees to sanctuary is that they are too old, or their health is too frail, and they might not survive the transfer. The decisions were based on reports by veterinarians working for the research facility, rather than by independent experts in chimpanzee care.[162]

In December 2022, a federal court ruled that NIH violated the CHIMP Act when it decided to keep chimpanzees at Alamogordo instead of transferring them to sanctuary.[163] United States District Judge Lydia Kay Griggsby ruled that the CHIMP Act is unambiguous in requiring that the NIH transfer all of its "retired" chimpanzees to sanctuary:

> This language makes clear that the Secretary of Health and Human Services, who has delegated this authority to NIH, "shall provide for the establishment and operation … of a system to provide for the lifetime care of chimpanzees." … The use of the word "shall" in subsection (c) of the CHIMP Act also makes clear that the requirement to transfer all surplus chimpanzees to sanctuary is a mandatory one.[164]

At the time of writing, the fate of the elderly chimpanzees remains in limbo. Since 2019, more than a dozen of the Alamogordo chimpanzees have died there, after spending their lives in a laboratory.[165] It is believed that more than thirty still remain.

It is important to remember that the poor health of these chimpanzees was caused by the trauma associated with their captivity, and by the procedures and experiments performed on them. Several are infected with HIV and hepatitis; some have had limbs amputated; most have heart disease. All of this is documented in the veterinarians' reports, which exploit these medical frailties to argue for keeping the chimpanzees imprisoned at Alamogordo. It is perverse to now deny the chimpanzees a chance at freedom, comfort, and security in their old age by claiming that the very harms visited upon them by research and captivity make them too frail to be released to sanctuary.

The story of these chimpanzees is one of multiple failures: the failure to recognize and respect their rights; the failure to replace chimpanzees with a more scientifically suitable method for studying HIV/AIDS and other infectious diseases (today, macaques are commonly used in HIV research, and some species are now endangered); the failure to provide for adequate, appropriate, and humane lifetime care. Their freedom, health, and lives have been sacrificed, and time is running out to repay the debt that is owed to them.

4 Justice

The third and final pillar of ethical research with NHPs is *justice*. Justice in research builds on the concept as defined in *The Belmont Report* and concerns the fair selection of research subjects. (It is common now to refer to human research subjects as "participants," but here we adhere to the older term "subjects" as it was used in *The Belmont Report*, in part to emphasize the moral commonalities between humans and NHPs. The latter are not properly called "participants" in scientific research.) To be just, the selection of research subjects must be based on demonstrable scientific need, not on convenience of acquisition or on the existence of relatively less rigorous regulatory requirements and oversight. The Council of Europe echoes this stance in its guidance on research with incarcerated persons: "Prisoners should never be chosen as the vehicle for experimentation simply as a consequence of the convenience of their situation."[166]

Historically, persons who were institutionalized, such as disabled children and adults, the elderly, and incarcerated and enslaved persons, were subjected to involuntary, harmful research owing to their ready availability and their inability to refuse or resist coercion (see Section 4.3). Responding to that manifest injustice, *The Belmont Report* called it unjust to use vulnerable research subjects for reasons of convenience rather than scientific need. For humans, this understanding of the requirements of justice means that researchers cannot use, in burdensome ways, vulnerable persons who are impoverished, incarcerated, or otherwise easy to access, coerce, and manipulate, and who cannot meaningfully consent or dissent.

4.1 Justice in *The Belmont Report*

Belmont does not offer a positive account of what justice requires, but rather points to historical injustices in research with human subjects to exemplify what cannot be consistent with just scientific research:

> For example, during the 19th and early 20th centuries the burdens of serving as research subjects fell largely upon poor ward patients, while the benefits of improved medical care flowed primarily to private patients. Subsequently, the exploitation of unwilling prisoners as research subjects in Nazi concentration camps was condemned as a particularly flagrant injustice. In this country, in the 1940's, the Tuskegee syphilis study used disadvantaged, rural black men to study the untreated course of a disease that is by no means confined to that population. These subjects were deprived of demonstrably effective treatment in order not to interrupt the project, long after such treatment became generally available.
>
> Against this historical background, it can be seen how conceptions of justice are relevant to research involving human subjects. For example, the selection of research subjects needs to be scrutinized in order to determine whether some classes (e.g., welfare patients, particular racial and ethnic minorities, or persons confined to institutions) are being systematically selected simply because of their easy availability, their compromised position, or their manipulability, rather than for reasons directly related to the problem being studied.[167]

We understand the *Belmont* principles as demanding that justice in science requires scientific justification – linking the ethical and scientific principles to their common origin in the Latin *justus* – while emphasizing that scientific justification can never override sound ethical constraints.

The conception of justice explicated in *Belmont* has been called "minimalist" by some critics, in that it seemingly reduces to the principles of respect for persons (or respecting the self-determination and autonomy of individuals), and beneficence/nonmaleficence (the obligation to maximize the benefits and minimize the harms of research). But this conception of beneficence in research is strained in the case of research with NHPs, who receive none of the benefits of most research, and most of the burdens and harms. Human-directed scientific activities involving NHPs are not fundamentally intended to benefit them, but rather to benefit humans, and to reduce the risks and harms to humans of research participation. It is understood that the risks and burdens to human research subjects can in principle be offset by benefits accrued to other, future human beneficiaries – in that sense, "beneficence is concerned with the distribution of benefits and burdens ... across different individuals."[168] Indeed, justice in *Belmont* is described as a matter of fair distribution of those benefits and burdens: "Who ought to receive the benefits of research and bear its burdens? This is a question of justice, in the sense of 'fairness in distribution' or 'what is deserved.' An injustice occurs when some benefit to which a person is entitled is denied without good reason or when some burden is imposed unduly."[169]

Belmont also explicitly conceives of the principle of justice as a requirement "that equals ought to be treated equally."[170] This entails that equal value and consideration should be assigned to each individual and their welfare, again linking justice to beneficence. In research, "Beneficence treats the space of equality as the domain of welfare – individuals have an equal claim to have their welfare be given equal weight to the welfare of everyone else."[171] Respect for persons does not simply reduce to beneficence either because it is also clearly concerned to accommodate whatever level of decisional competence a subject possesses (and not just protect them from exploitation and harm).[172]

Justice, respect for persons, and beneficence are not fully discrete principles in *Belmont*, as each aims to protect the vulnerable. Beneficence requires scientific justification for using the vulnerable, while justice requires fairness in the selection of subjects. Respect for persons requires voluntary consent, either of a subject or their guardian/surrogate, while justice protects against the exploitation of those who are dependent or unrepresented. Justice is therefore not fully reducible to beneficence, for even a scientifically justifiable use of a vulnerable subject can be impermissible if it unfairly exploits them by taking advantage of their accessibility and ease of use (see Section 4.3).

Justice specifically constrains the use of vulnerable subjects for reasons of convenience.

4.2 Why Nonhuman Primates Are Subjects of Justice

As a grounding moral principle guiding science with living animals, the principle of equal treatment requires and justifies harmonization of research guidelines and principles governing human and nonhuman research. Thus, we argue, the principle of justice as described in *Belmont* should and does apply to NHPs, and the fair distribution of the benefits and burdens of research encompasses both human and nonhuman research subjects.

Nonhuman primates are used in harmful scientific activities that are not permitted with humans. What was once true of vulnerable human subjects is true today of NHPs, who are used in science because they are readily available and relatively unprotected (see Section 1.5). Like other captive subjects who are dependent on their captors for their survival, vulnerable to coercion, and not free to leave, NHPs can be made to comply in experiments, but they cannot consent or even meaningfully dissent to being used in research and their expressions of dissent (e.g., trying to escape, withdrawing from the scientist or technician, expressing distress when immobilized) are ignored and suppressed.[173] In other words, they are systematically selected because they are available and manipulable. And NHPs are used despite mounting scientific evidence of their unsuitability as models of humans and human disorders. That is, they are used for reasons not "directly related to the problem being studied."[174] NHPs are used because nontherapeutic research methods, which include surgical procedures, infection, inflicted traumatic injuries, implantation with brain electrodes and other devices, amputation, restraint, captivity, psychological trauma, and death, are rightly prohibited with human research subjects. The use of NHPs, in other words, is a matter of administrative convenience rather than scientific necessity. As discussed, the translational failure of NHP research provides evidence that their continued use is not scientifically justified. But even if it were scientifically justifiable, justice considerations would not sanction their use (see Section 4.3). Thus, lax regulations for animal use coupled with strong regulations for the protection of human research subjects have led to overreliance on NHPs and other animals because it is simply easier and possible to use them.

The use of NHPs in research is not justified by scientific need, but rather by restrictions that limit the use of humans and perceptions that other animals, like NHPs, are not due similar moral regard. This is similar to the use, historically, of marginalized, disadvantaged, and disempowered human populations for the benefit of more advantageously situated persons. This justification for using NHPs, as we have argued, is inadequate in part because it fails to consider the morally relevant similarities between humans and NHPs that require human-similar moral consideration for NHPs – it fails to treat equals equally. But justice in research as we conceive it requires both ethical justification and a robust and empirically informed, defensible scientific justification. It requires making a scientific case for using a NHP in a proposed research project. That scientific case cannot consider nonscientific factors like the ready availability of NHPs, or the more restrictive regulations on using human subjects. It must, however, consider previous scientific studies with NHPs, including research that has already answered the questions asked by the proposed use, as well as evidence of the unsuitability of NHPs as models of humans and human disorders. It must make the case for using NHPs instead of humans on scientific grounds. And it must consider the existence of comparable or superior alternatives to using NHPs. As discussed in Section 3.3, using other nonhuman animals instead of NHPs is not a morally defensible alternative. Indeed, NHPs are frequently the "translational" model used before research shifts to human subjects owing to their genetic and biological proximity to humans, which serves to highlight the extent of the justification problem for using other animals as well.

Using NHPs because they are more convenient and easier to use than human subjects, and not because they are the best scientific models, violates the principle of justice. To be just, research with NHPs must be scientifically informed and evidence-based and conform with our highest ethical standards. That requires learning from past failures and recognizing the potential scientific value of methods that can replace the use of NHPs. Applying the same care and rigor to NHP research as is applied to human research will improve science and enhance its benefits. It must start with the just and scientifically informed selection of subjects. Judged by that standard, *nearly all current research with NHPs is unjust and should be prohibited.*

Some scientific activities involving NHPs pass the test of justice. For example, research that observes the behavior of free-living NHPs, the analysis of samples (such as fecal samples or shed/discarded biological materials like hair or food) acquired without interfering with the animals, necropsies on animals who have died, and existing cell lines and cultures can all be conducted without violating the principle of justice. Similar research on NHPs living in sanctuaries that provide, as far as possible, the conditions necessary for their flourishing can also be conducted without being unjust. Such research might be beneficial to the animals studied, or it might be motivated by curiosity. It would add to what is known about diverse NHPs and might also add to our understanding of humans and human behaviors.

4.3 Spotlight: The Willowbrook Hepatitis Experiments

Willowbrook was a residential state school for children with developmental disabilities in Staten Island, New York. In 1955, Dr. Saul Krugman began a fourteen-year experiment on the children of Willowbrook, infecting them with hepatitis to test the effects of gamma globulin antibodies. Because of the unsanitary conditions at Willowbrook, infection with hepatitis, a viral disease of the liver, was common. Krugman claimed that there was a 90 percent infection rate, although contemporary estimates put it closer to 30–50 percent.[175] Parents of the children were told they would be part of an experiment that would potentially offer lifelong immunity to hepatitis. They were not told their children would be fed live virus through food contaminated with feces.

The unsanitary conditions and overcrowding at Willowbrook were responsible for frequent outbreaks of disease, including hepatitis, shigellosis, and parasitic and respiratory infections. Krugman's research yielded valuable information. He discovered that there were two different strains of hepatitis endemic at Willowbrook: hepatitis A, which causes jaundice, fever, nausea and diarrhea, and hepatitis B, which causes more serious, chronic illness. Krugman also discovered that hepatitis A was transmitted through the fecal–oral route, while hepatitis B was transmitted through blood and sexual contact. Finally, Krugman developed a prototype vaccine against hepatitis B, using inactivated virus from the blood plasma of infected children.

Krugman genuinely believed that any harms caused by his research were fully justified by the benefits to humanity as a whole, and defended the experiments for the rest of his life. Nonetheless, when Krugman published early results from his studies in 1958, there was immediate controversy about the ethics of using institutionalized children with developmental disabilities. One of the criticisms was that although Willowbrook employed nearly 1,000 adults, including 600 ward attendants who were also frequently exposed to hepatitis, Krugman did not experiment on any of them. Another criticism was that Krugman exploited the poor conditions at Willowbrook that led to frequent infections, and used captive children whose parents had little choice but to send them to a poorly run public institution. (At the time, it was common for children with developmental disabilities to be institutionalized.) In a letter published in *The Lancet*, Dr. Stephen Goldby wrote: "The duty of a pediatrician in a situation such as exists at Willowbrook State School is to attempt to improve that situation, not to turn it to his advantage for experimental purposes, however lofty the aims."[176] Theologian and bioethicist Paul Ramsey was a vocal critic of the experiments. He said "children in institutions and not directly under the care of parents or relatives should never be used in medical investigations having present pain or discomfort and unknown present and future risks to them, and promising future possible benefits only for others."[177] Vaccinologist Maurice Hilleman called the Willowbrook studies "the most unethical medical experiments ever performed on children in the United States."[178]

The Willowbrook experiments ended in 1970, and profoundly influenced the work of the Belmont Commission, whose *Belmont Report* laid the ethical foundations for US regulations on research with human subjects. One of the most important insights of *The Belmont Report* concerns its definition of justice as the fair selection of subjects based on genuine scientific need and suitability rather than on convenience. It is unjust, *The Belmont Report* says, to use institutionalized children and other vulnerable persons merely because it is convenient and easy to exploit them. Moreover, *Belmont* states that the possible benefits to others cannot justify exploiting the vulnerable. This can be viewed as a direct attack on the Willowbrook experiments, and on Krugman's arguments that the benefits to society outweighed the harms he inflicted on the children there.

The Willowbrook State School was finally shut down in 1987 after several news reports brought attention to the filthy, neglectful conditions in the institution. Survivors of Willowbrook were transferred to community homes, and the scandals associated with the school led to the passage of the federal Civil Rights of Institutionalized Persons Act of 1980.[179]

The lessons of Willowbrook for scientific studies with NHPs are clear. As critics of the Willowbrook experiments argued, the possible benefits to other humans did not justify exploiting Willowbrook's vulnerable children. Even experiments that contribute important knowledge to medical science *can be unethical*. Similarly, the possible benefits to humans cannot make the exploitation of NHPs right. Nonhuman primates continue to be used in harmful research on hepatitis and other infectious diseases including SARS-CoV-2, but the necessity of using them, and their actual contributions to advances in human health are unclear, even when the research program overall appears to achieve its goals (see Section 5.1). Nonhuman primates and human children ought to be treated alike for research purposes, because both groups are vulnerable to harm, coercion, and exploitation and are not able to protect their own rights against being experimented upon. If what happened to the children of Willowbrook was wrong – and it most definitely was – it is wrong today to exploit NHPs in the same way.

5 The Path Forward

It is possible that it is scientifically, ethically, and socially important and necessary to study a scientific problem, and that it is also ethically wrong to use NHPs to study that problem. This same dilemma occurs in research with human subjects. The increasing use of NHPs and other sentient nonhuman animals has, for decades, been a response to ethical concerns about and restrictions on scientific activities involving humans. The global scientific community was able to successfully pivot from research that unjustly exploited vulnerable humans in the twentieth century. This is compelling evidence of the flexibility and ingenuity of science and scientists when faced with both scientific, ethical, and legal challenges. That kind of flexibility and ingenuity has led to the development of nonanimal and human-biology-based technologies and methods, and it must be directed with all deliberate speed toward ending the unjust exploitation of NHPs in science.

There are two mutually viable paths forward. The first, harmonization, would be imposed on science and scientists from the outside, by governments, by societies, and by funders. Harmonization alone would not rule out all research on and with NHPs, just as human research guidelines do not completely rule out using children, incarcerated persons, or other vulnerable persons. Harmonization means that additional protections and restrictions that are similar, but typically not greater than those required for vulnerable humans, would be provided to NHPs. This change would be impactful and challenging, but science and scientists rose to a similar challenge in the past, notably in the twentieth century when human research and animal welfare regulations were developed and enacted in response to public outcry over abuses. Harmonization requires that we go further than the minimal and permissive animal welfare regulations that currently exist, with the result that many of the scientific practices and methods currently permitted will no longer be allowed. It is probable that most of the scientific activities currently involving NHPs would be prohibited by harmonization. Science and scientists have proven in the past that they can innovate and work in less permissive environments, and they should be called on to do so again.

The second pathway is widely and voluntarily replacing NHPs with human-relevant alternatives. This pathway provides a solution to the ethical problems posed by NHP scientific activities that the sciences can control and impose on themselves as both a scientific and an ethical imperative. Replacement depends on the creativity, ingenuity, and know-how of scientists. They have already demonstrated the possibility and viability of this way forward, with numerous advances over the last decade. Replacing NHPs with human-relevant technologies is now possible due to those advances, and it should be a priority for any science and scientists genuinely committed to justice and to high quality, beneficial, human-relevant research. Given the history of science, it is likely that some scientific communities will only change when they are legally required to do so. And, to be fair, in some areas of animal use (e.g., toxicology), legal regulations must change to allow scientific innovations that replace NHPs. But change that only comes through the force of law, as happened in the twentieth century with science using human subjects, is only necessary in the face of unreasonable intransigence. We hope for better from scientific communities.

The Three Pillars of *harmonization*, *replacement*, and *justice* will together rule out harmful scientific studies and uses of NHPs. Specifically, anything that is not permitted when using human subjects, including methods that cause pain, suffering, distress, and injury; nonbeneficial procedures; and intentional death will be prohibited in scientific activities involving NHPs. Eliminating that kind of science will have the effect of reducing the purported need and demand for NHPs; they are currently used in science specifically because those methods are prohibited in humans.

5.1 Spotlight: A Tale of Two Pandemics – Polio and COVID

In the early twentieth century, severe poliomyelitis (polio) outbreaks in the United States and Europe were common. In humans, polio is a virus that can cause paralysis and death by targeting the central nervous system. United States President Franklin D. Roosevelt had polio, and in 1938 he founded the National Foundation for Infantile Paralysis (NFIP) which funded research to combat polio and develop an effective vaccine. The NFIP played a crucial role in securing an enormous number of rhesus macaques, through a global network of "monkey dealers," for researchers experimenting with polio.

The development of the polio vaccine is frequently cited by animal scientists as one of the great triumphs of animal research, and proof that animal research is necessary for the protection of human health. The polio vaccine has been a major scientific and public health success, virtually eradicating the disease in most parts of the world and preventing deaths and acquired disabilities. But the research leading to the polio vaccines took place nearly seventy years ago and, in the decades since, it has become clear that while a great deal of biomedical research does *use* animals, it is not necessarily true that the research programs succeeded *because* of animal research. It may have been possible to achieve those successes *without* the use of animals.[180]

From the 1930s to the 1950s, hundreds of thousands of wild-caught rhesus monkeys were exported to the United States from India for the "war against polio." The monkeys were used because they were susceptible to polio infection and had neurological symptoms similar to those seen in humans. (NHPs, including chimpanzees, are also susceptible to wild polio infection.) For the research, monkeys were infected with viral material obtained from humans. Researchers used the monkeys' susceptibility to polio to model the human disease and differentiate between strains. They also cultivated poliovirus in monkeys to formulate and test vaccines prior to human trials.[181]

The use of monkeys changed the course of polio research, but not always for the better. The discovery that polio is caused by a virus is attributed to Simon Flexner, a scientist who showed that it could be transmitted between monkeys. But Flexner's experiments with rhesus monkeys contributed to a misleading understanding of polio, because he used a species that is not infected orally and is not susceptible to the less deadly intestinal disease caused by the virus. Early efforts to develop a polio vaccine involved using a killed virus taken from rhesus monkey spinal cords. The monkeys were infected with polio, then killed, and their spinal cords "squeezed out," but a single monkey could yield enough viral material for only about ten doses.[182] Researchers sought presidential intervention to ensure adequate supplies of monkeys for the gruesome work. However, the vaccines produced in this way were not safe. One trial of a killed-virus vaccine, tested in several thousand children, resulted in allergic reactions and potential infections with polio. A similar vaccine that used live virus from monkeys resulted in several deaths and polio infections.[183]

The monkeys used in the "war against polio" endured capture, months-long journeys aboard ships, and lengthy quarantines before the survivors reached their final destinations: the laboratories where they would be infected with polio and killed. The exportation of thousands of these monkeys in the 1940s caused alarm in India, and legislators, members of parliament, Hindu and Jain organizations, and anti-vivisectionist groups protested.[184] Indian government restrictions on exports during hot weather months, prompted by concerns about the welfare of monkeys transported during those periods, caused some US researchers to declare an "emergency" shortage of monkeys. At the same time, the medical director of the NFIP, in a letter with racist overtones, blamed "ignorant natives in India and completely untrained persons on board ship" for the poor health of the monkeys it acquired.[185]

By the end of the 1940s, polio researchers had successfully cultivated poliovirus in non-neurological human tissues acquired from hospitals, including fetal tissue from stillbirths and miscarriages.[186] This research was a game changer for the development of the polio vaccine. It overturned the previous belief, based on monkey experiments, that the virus only attacked the nervous system, and could only be grown in neurological tissue, and it was essential to vaccine development. The cell culture method allowed scientists to combine different strains of the virus with serum antibodies in test tubes. Poliovirus could be grown and replicated without using monkeys, and it was possible to culture large quantities of virus, which paved the way for the polio vaccines.[187] Officials at the NFIP, who had previously lobbied for tens of thousands of living monkeys, heralded the scientific breakthrough as "the end of the monkey era."[188] That declaration was premature, and today, many tens of thousands of monkeys are still used in science.

Hundreds of thousands of monkeys died during scientific experimentation on polio. While it is very clear that many monkeys were *used* in that research, what is less clear is how critical they were to the most important discoveries about polio. The use of specific types of monkeys may actually have held back scientific progress. Human research subjects, injected with vaccines from monkey-derived viruses, were harmed, and some died. In the end, one of the most significant innovations to come out of polio research was the development of human-based cell cultures that are today widely used in many kinds of research, including cancer and Alzheimer's research, and in toxicology testing.[189]

In early 2020, the global COVID-19 pandemic sparked a new race to discover a vaccine against a deadly virus. This time, researchers were able to rapidly develop safe and effective vaccines by fast-tracking COVID-19 research and emphasizing human clinical trials over lengthy experiments with animals.[190] At the time, the US Food & Drug Administration (FDA) still required animal testing of new drugs prior to approval, so animal testing of the vaccines was performed at the same time as human trials, as well as after the vaccines were approved for humans under an Emergency Use Authorization. This was a case of regulatory and bureaucratic box-ticking. In 2022, the US Congress passed the FDA Modernization Act 2.0, which permits the use of nonanimal alternatives to test the safety and efficacy of new drugs and removes the requirement for animal testing prior to approval of biosimilar drugs.[191]

Today, as in the 1930s, scientists claim there is a critical monkey shortage, which specifically threatens vaccine research, including COVID-19 vaccine research.[192] Yet, there is evidence that the macaques used in COVID-19 research are not good models – an example of the high fidelity fallacy, in which animals with a stronger resemblance to humans are believed to be better models.[193] Decades after the war against polio was won, scientific progress in developing alternatives to using animals has been slowed by the lack of scientific interest, and funding, for such research. Yet the war against polio yielded not only effective vaccines, but also a truly beneficial alternative to infecting monkeys with the virus: human tissue cultures that are based on human rather than monkey biology. Confronting the so-called monkey shortage today requires the same innovation that was shown by scientists in the 1940s. Scientific innovation and discovery can improve science and make human-directed research on NHPs – and diseases like polio – a thing of the past.

5.2 The End of the Monkey Era

Scientists who use animals in scientific activities often say they look forward to the day when it is no longer necessary to use animals. For example, the chemical company SC Johnson, which continues to test its products on animals, states: "We look forward to a day when there's no more animal testing."[194] Yet, such words are empty and disingenuous if not paired with effective actions, such as lobbying legislative and regulatory bodies for changes in regulations and funding priorities, working to develop viable and effective alternatives, and using more creative scientific methods that will not cause harm to animals.[195] Moreover, both the increased scale and scope of the use of animals, including NHPs, in scientific activities suggests a lack of commitment to ensuring that day comes. The Three Pillars describes both ethical and epistemic responsibilities of scientists. These are responsibilities to the societies that entrust them with funding and resources to pursue beneficial research in the public interest, and to the animals they continue to exploit. The Three Pillars responds to twenty-first-century science, and recognizes that the goals of the Three Rs have neither been fully achieved, nor, in far too many instances, have they been sincerely or adequately pursued. Nonhuman primates have not been replaced with nonsentient alternatives, even as the science of human-relevant nonanimal methods has progressed, and in spite of evidence that NHPs are not good scientific models for uniquely human disorders, injuries, or disabilities. Despite more sophisticated understanding of the psychosocial and physical needs of NHPs, the conditions in which they are held captive have scarcely improved – they continue to be housed in barren steel cages, alone, isolated, and bored (see Sections 2.6 and 2.7).[196] They continue to suffer pain and distress in the name of science, notwithstanding the Three Rs putative commitment to refinement (see Section 1.5).[197] Moreover, the expanded scope and scale of the use of NHPs in scientific activities since the 1950s has helped drive some commonly used species, like long-tailed and pig-tailed macaques, toward extinction (see Sections 1.2 and 1.3). None of this portends an end to the use of NHPs in harmful science and research.

It is no longer a reasonably disputed claim that humanity has reached a turning point in how we live on this planet. The global anthropogenic climate and ecological crises, both independent of one another and yet partially entangled (e.g., habitat loss resulting from expanding animal-based agriculture), are of our own making and result from, among other things, short-sighted policies, regulations, toxic nationalism, toxic value systems, and groupthink. For our societies to survive as we currently know them, change must happen. This change has to better come to terms with the detrimental effects of human supremacist attitudes, values, beliefs, laws, and regulations. The Three Pillars is strongly anchored in a wholesale rejection of human supremacy. We think that such a rejection, so crucial to the continued survival of our current societies, must impact how we use animals in science (along with other domains of animal use). Two crucial questions to ask at this point are: *What kinds of societies do we want to live in? What kinds of societal attitudes and values can we no longer afford to hold?*

The Three Pillars calls for a radical rethink of the use of NHPs, modeled on well-established and widely endorsed international guidelines and principles for research with captive, institutionalized, and vulnerable human subjects, and consistent with the foundational moral principle of treating equals equally. Scientists who use NHPs have accepted, tacitly or explicitly, that they are physiologically, genetically, and psychologically similar enough to humans to serve as substitutes in harmful, invasive, and lethal scientific studies. Those similarities are only part of the picture. Nonhuman primates are similar to humans in other equally important ways: in their complex and varied social and familial structures, in their culture, communication, tool use, emotions, and in their capacity to teach and learn. They are similar to humans, in short, in many of the ways that make humans the subjects of morality and of justice. The moral imperative to protect NHPs from the harms and abuses of research is clear.

The astute reader will have noticed that what we say here about NHPs applies equally to other nonhuman animals used in science. While the specific capacities and vulnerabilities of other nonhuman animals will differ with their physiological, psychological, and cognitive differences, none of the traits and capacities that are associated with moral status in humans are *unique* to humans. Across species and taxa, including phylogenetically distant species like octopuses and fishes, other animals will exhibit some, many, perhaps most of those valued traits and capacities. Logically, consistently, what the Three Pillars calls on us to do for NHPs, it also calls on us to do for those other animals who are used in science as well. The implications for science of the Three Pillars are clear and imperative.

Notes

The Three Pillars of Ethical Research with Nonhuman Primates

1. Grimm 2020; Ferdowsian & Johnson 2022; Grimm 2023; Peat 2023; Wang & Yaun 2023.
2. Grimm 2018; Zhang 2020; Shapiro et al. 2022.
3. Collins 2015.
4. Reardon 2019; Grimm 2020; Neergaard 2023.
5. Kinter et al. 2021.
6. World Medical Association 1964.
7. While we do not explicitly consider animals held in zoos or used for entertainment or for food, it bears noting that many of the harms we describe in what follows are also experienced by those animals as well, and, of course, there is animal-based science focused on the animals bred, raised, or kept in those domains of animal use.
8. Engber 2009; European Commission 2010; Transportation, Sale, and Handling of Certain Animals 2011.
9. European Commission 2010.
10. When we refer to the use of NHPs in research and science as *human-directed*, we mean use that is intended to benefit humans and human interests. It is those, and other harmful uses, on which we are primarily focused in this Element, though some of our analyses and comments apply more broadly.
11. Weintraub 2019; Hamzelou 2023.
12. National Institutes of Health 2019; Brain/MINDS 2021.
13. US Department of Agriculture (APHIS) 2013.
14. Grimm 2018; US Department of Agriculture (APHIS) 2021.
15. New England Primate Conservancy 2021.
16. Pound et al. 2004; Bailey & Taylor 2009; Institue of Medicine (US) and National Research Council (US) 2011; European Commission 2017; US Government Accounting Office 2019.
17. Zhang 2020.
18. National Academies of Sciences, Engineering, and Medicine 2022.
19. National Academies of Sciences, Engineering, and Medicine 2023.
20. National Academies of Sciences, Engineering, and Medicine 2023, 152.
21. Robitzski 2022.
22. National Academies of Sciences, Engineering, and Medicine 2023, 89.
23. Robitzski 2022.
24. Robitzski 2022.
25. Qi, Stepniewska, & Kaas 2000; Williams-Blangero, VandeBerg, & Dyke 2002; Kaas & Qi 2004; Griffith & Humphrey 2006; Pluchino et al. 2009; Marthas et al. 2011; Leblanc et al. 2013; Ferdowsian & Fuentes 2014; Kishi et al. 2014; Schwarz et al. 2014; Cyranoski 2019; Liu et al. 2019; Urano et al. 2021; Hawthorne et al. 2022; O'Dell 2022. Oikonomidis et al 2017; Brutcher 2013.

26. Collin et al. 1982.
27. Ferdowsian et al. 2022.
28. Levenson 2022; Gamillo 2023.
29. European Commission 2010; Stanford Medicine 2023.
30. Can, D'Cruze, & Macdonald 2019.
31. Can, D'Cruze, & Macdonald 2019; Rush, Dale, & Aguirre 2021.
32. Can, D'Cruze, & Macdonald 2019; Warne, Moloney, & Chaber 2023.
33. Robitzski 2022.
34. Warne, Moloney, & Chaber 2023.
35. Hansen et al. 2022a.
36. Hansen et al. 2021, 5.
37. Grimm 2022b.
38. Warne, Moloney, & Chaber 2023.
39. Warne, Moloney, & Chaber 2023.
40. Hansen et al. 2022b.
41. Animal Welfare Institute 2022.
42. Kevany & Colley 2023; Malisow 2023.
43. Hansen et al. 2021; Colley 2023.
44. Maldonado & Peck 2014.
45. Maldonado & Peck 2014.
46. Fernandez-Duque et al. 2020.
47. Maldonado & Peck 2014.
48. Suleman et al. 2004.
49. Fernström et al. 2008, 468.
50. National Research Council 2006, 104.
51. National Research Council 2006.
52. Fernström et al. 2008.
53. Can, D'Cruze, & Macdonald 2019; Colley 2023; Warne, Moloney, & Chaber 2023.
54. For more on formal justice, see Gosepath 2021; Miller 2021.
55. Rachels & Rachels 1986.
56. Bateson 2011; Conlee & Rowan 2012; Redmond 2012; Arnason & Clausen 2016; Bradley et al. 2020.
57. Conlee & Rowan 2012.
58. De Waal & Preston 2017.
59. Moll et al. 2007.
60. De Waal & Preston 2017.
61. Anderson et al. 2017; De Waal & Preston 2017.
62. De Waal & Preston 2017.
63. Harlow & Suomi 1974; Rasmussen & Reite 1982.
64. *The Belmont Report* (1979) laid the ethical groundwork for US human research regulations. Written by a national commission, the report established three core principles to guide research with human subjects. The first is Respect for Persons, which is operationalized as a requirement that research participation should be voluntary, and that subjects (or their authorized surrogates) must provide informed consent. The second is

Beneficence, an obligation to do no harm, and to maximize the benefits and minimize the harms of research. Beneficence is operationalized by the assessment of risks and benefits in justifying research, and prohibits the brutal or inhumane treatment of human subjects, including intentional killing and infliction of significant harm. Beneficence importantly requires that the use of vulnerable persons is scientifically justified, linking it to the third principle, Justice, which is the fair selection of research subjects. Justice requires both scientific and ethical justification for the selection of research subjects, and is specifically intended to protect vulnerable humans from exploitation and overuse in research simply because they are easily accessed and manipulated. Under *Belmont*'s conception of justice, even potentially beneficial research can be ethically impermissible and prohibited because it exploits vulnerable individuals or populations. See National Commission for the Protection of Human Subjects of Biomedical and Behavioral Research 1979; Beauchamp 2008.

65. Ferdowsian et al 2020.
66. Association for Psychological Science 2018.
67. Association for Psychological Science 2018.
68. Phillips 2014.
69. Wisconsin National Primate Research Center 2023.
70. Reardon 2015.
71. King 2015.
72. Grimm 2022a; Wang & Yaun 2023.
73. Frank 2005; Faunalytics 2008; Lohse 2021; Safer Medicines 2021.
74. Weatherall, Goodfellow, & Harris 2006; Institute of Medicine (US) and National Research Council (US) 2011; European Commission 2017; National Academies of Sciences, Engineering, and Medicine 2023.
75. Weatherall, Goodfellow, & Harris 2006.
76. Russell & Burch 1959.
77. Council for International Organizations of Medical Sciences 2016, 57.
78. National Commission 1979, sect. 3.
79. Owens 2013.
80. Hayward et al. 2021; Perreault 2022; Canadian Institutes of Health Research 2022.
81. United Nations 1988, Principle 22.
82. Council of Europe Committee of Ministers 1995.
83. See Fenton 2014 for more on how this relates to animal dissent.
84. Pound et al. 2004; Bailey & Taylor 2009; Institute of Medicine (US) and National Research Council (US) 2011; European Commission 2017; Solis-Moreira 2021.
85. European Commission 2010.
86. European Commission 2010.
87. Baker 2016, 783.
88. Institute of Medicine 2011.
89. Tyson 2021.
90. Institute of Medicine (US) and National Research Council (US) 2011, 16.

91. Schroeder et al. 2018.
92. Schroeder et al. 2018.
93. Schroeder 2018; Schroeder 2019; Chatfield et al. 2021; Nature Magazine 2022.
94. Jacobs 2020a; Diamond 2001; Pomerantz, Meiri, & Terkel 2013; Poirier & Bateson 2017; Jacobs 2020b.
95. Russell & Burch 1959.
96. Canadian Council on Animal Care 1993; National Centre for the Replacement, Refinement & Reduction of Animals in Research 2017.
97. Russell & Burch 1959; Herrmann, Pistollato, & Stephens 2019.
98. Solis-Moreira 2021.
99. Knight 2007.
100. National Institutes of Health Veterinary Panel 2019.
101. Canadian Council on Animal Care 1993.
102. Russell & Burch 1959, 3–4.
103. Safer Medicines 2021.
104. Shook 2022.
105. National Primate Research Centers.
106. US Government Accounting Office 2019.
107. National Institutes of Health 2020.
108. Johnson 2020a, 180.
109. Imanis Life Sciences 2021.
110. Bailey, Balcomb, & Capaldo 2007; Knight 2007; Garner 2014; Akhtar 2015.
111. Garner 2014, 438.
112. Garner 2014.
113. Sun 2022.
114. McManus 2013, 7.
115. O'Collins et al. 2006, 467.
116. Xu & Pan 2013.
117. National Institute of Neurological Disorders and Stroke 2014.
118. Johnson 2020b.
119. Traystman 2003; Cook & Tymianski 2012; National Institute of Neurological Disorders and Stroke 2014.
120. Bailey 2005; Bailey & Taylor 2016.
121. American Museum of Natural History 2019; Suntsova & Buzdin 2020; Turner 2023.
122. Bailey 2009, 408.
123. Bailey 2009, 407.
124. Bailey 2009, 407.
125. Bailey 2009, 409.
126. Knight 2007.
127. Knight 2007, 294.
128. Knight 2007, 295.
129. Knight 2007, 302.
130. Bailey 2014.

131. Bailey 2014, 304.
132. Barouch et al. 2002; Watkins et al. 2008; Cohen 2020.
133. Sekaly 2008.
134. Sekaly 2008.
135. Shanks & Greek 2008, 1012.
136. Bailey 2005, 235.
137. Pamies & Hartung 2017, 43.
138. Traystman 2003; O'Collins et al. 2006; Cook & Tymianski 2012; Xu & Pan 2013; Johnson 2020b.
139. Carbone 2014.
140. Keim 2023.
141. Birke, Arluke, & Michael 2007.
142. Schroeder et al. 2018.
143. Institute of Medicine (US) and National Research Council (US) 2011, 16.
144. Institute of Medicine (US) and National Research Council (US) 2011, 16.
145. Institute of Medicine (US) and National Research Council (US) 2011, 23.
146. Canadian Council on Animal Care 1993.
147. Braithwaite & Huntingford 2004; Sneddon & Brown 2020.
148. We can envision three responses to translational failure that seek to maintain the status quo: (1) a denial of this failure (or at least of its significance), (2) an acknowledgment of this failure but with an eye to modifying the design of animal studies, and (3) an acknowledgement of this failure but with an eye to modifying the *animals* to be used in animal studies. When they are not denying translational failure (or its significance), pro-animal research sites or scholars tend to favor defending better designed animal-based studies (the PREPARE and ARRIVE Guidelines reflect these efforts, as do the STAIR Guidelines mentioned in Section 3.1). The third option, modifying the animals, has been used for some time to "humanize" animal models (e.g., the many transgenic mice developed for scientific use, as well as genetically modified monkeys that have been developed to purportedly study numerous human disorders, including Alzheimer's disease). See National Centre for the Replacement, Refinement & Reduction of Animals in Research 2017; Smith et al. 2018; ARRIVE Guidelines 2020.
149. Iritani et al. 2018; Zhao, Jiang, & Zhang 2018.
150. Crozier et al. 2020; Johnson 2023.
151. German Ethics Council, 2011, 28.
152. Greely et al. 2007.
153. Johnson 2023, 260.
154. Rollin 2009.
155. National Research Council 1997; Bailey 2008.
156. National Institutes of Health 2013.
157. United States Fish and Wildlife Service 2015.
158. Collins 2015.
159. Chimpanzee Health Improvement, Maintenance, and Protection Act 2000.
160. Chimpanzee Health Improvement, Maintenance, and Protection Act 2000.
161. Last1000chimps.com 2021.

162. National Institutes of Health Veterinary Panel 2019.

163. Candelaria 2022.

164. *The Humane Society of the United States et al.* v. *National Institutes of Health et al.* 2023.

165. Maxwell 2022.

166. Council of Europe 1987.

167. National Commission for the Protection of Human Subjects of Biomedical and Behavioral Research 1979, part B: 3.

168. London 2021, 54.

169. National Commission for the Protection of Human Subjects of Biomedical and Behavioral Research 1979, part B: 3.

170. National Commission for the Protection of Human Subjects of Biomedical and Behavioral Research 1979.

171. London 2021, 55.

172. National Commission for the Protection of Human Subjects of Biomedical and Behavioral Research 1979; Beauchamp 2008.

173. Carbone 2004; Fenton 2014; Fenton 2019; London 2021, 55.

174. Solis-Moreira 2021.

175. Krugman 1986; Robinson 2008.

176. Goldby 1971.

177. Ramsey 2002, 55.

178. Offit 2007, 27.

179. Civil Rights of Institutionalized Persons Act 1980.

180. Pound et al. 2004.

181. Suri 2022.

182. Suri 2022.

183. Suri 2022.

184. Suri 2022.

185. Gudakunst 1940.

186. Smith 1990.

187. Barnes 2020.

188. Suri 2022.

189. Hartung 2009.

190. Boodman 2020.

191. FDA Modernization Act 2.0 2022.

192. Zhang 2020; National Academies of Sciences, Engineering, and Medicine 2023.

193. Fenton & Johnson 2020.

194. SC Johnson 2019.

195. For more on nonanimal methods, see Kandárová & Letašiová 2011; Herrmann, Pistollato. & Stephens 2019; National Toxicology Program 2024; Animal Free Research UK.

196. Institute of Medicine (US) and National Research Council (US) 2011; Johnson 2020a.

197. Reinhardt, Liss, & Stevens 1995; Balcombe, Barnard, & Sandusky 2004; Novak et al. 2013.

References

Akhtar A. The flaws and human harms of animal experimentation. *Cambridge Quarterly of Healthcare Ethics*. 2015 Oct;24(4):407–19.

American Museum of Natural History. DNA: Comparing humans and chimps. 2019. https://bit.ly/3QO9TBg.

Anderson JR, Bucher B, Chijiiwa H, Kuroshima H, Takimoto A, Fujita K. Third-party social evaluations of humans by monkeys and dogs. *Neuroscience & Biobehavioral Reviews*. 2017 Nov;82:95–109.

Animal Free Research UK. Completed projects. Website. www.animalfreere searchuk.org/completed-projects/.

Animal Welfare Institute. AWI urges US government to suspend purchases from monkey suppliers after smuggling indictment. *AWI Quarterly*. 2022;71(4):20–21.

Arnason G, Clausen J. On balance: Weighing harms and benefits in fundamental neurological research using nonhuman primates. *Medicine, Health Care and Philosophy*. 2016 Jun;19:229–37.

ARRIVE Guidelines. Website. 2020. https://arriveguidelines.org/about.

Association for Psychological Science. Harlow's classic studies revealed the importance of maternal contact. 2018 Jun 20. https://bit.ly/3QMuoON.

Bailey J. Non-human primates in medical research and drug development: A critical review. *Biogenic Amines*. 2005 Dec;19(4):235–55.

Bailey J. An assessment of the role of chimpanzees in AIDS vaccine research. *Alternatives to Laboratory Animals*. 2008 Sep;36(4):381–428. https://doi .org/10.1177/026119290803600403.

Bailey J. An examination of chimpanzee use in human cancer research. *Alternatives to Laboratory Animals*. 2009 Sep;37(4):399–416.

Bailey J. Monkey-based research on human disease: The implications of genetic differences. *Alternatives to Laboratory Animals*. 2014 Nov;42(5):287–317.

Bailey J, Taylor K. The SCHER report on non-human primate research – biased and deeply flawed. *Alternatives to Laboratory Animals*. 2009 Sep;37(4): 427–35.

Bailey J, Taylor K. Non-human primates in neuroscience research: The case against its scientific necessity. *Alternatives to Laboratory Animals*. 2016 Mar;44(1):43–69.

Bailey J, Balcombe J, Capaldo T. Chimpanzee research: An examination of its contribution to biomedical knowledge and efficacy in combating human diseases. Well-Being International, Experimentation Collection. 2007 Jan 1. www.wellbeingintlstudiesrepository.org/acwp_arte/129/.

Baker KC. Survey of 2014 behavioral management programs for laboratory primates in the United States. *American Journal of Primatology.* 2016 Jul;78(7):780–96.

Balcombe JP, Barnard ND, Sandusky C. Laboratory routines cause animal stress. *Journal of the American Association for Laboratory Animal Science.* 2004 Nov;43(6):42–51.

Barnes K. Culturing poliovirus in cells. *Nature Research.* 2020 Sep 28. www .nature.com/articles/d42859-020-00014-7.

Barouch DH, Kunstman J, Kuroda MJ, Schmitz JE, Santra S, Peyerl FW, Krivulka GR, Beaudry K, Lifton MA, Gorgone DA, Montefiori DC. Eventual AIDS vaccine failure in a rhesus monkey by viral escape from cytotoxic T lymphocytes. *Nature.* 2002 Jan;415(6869):335–39.

Bateson PJ-B, Johansen-Berg H, Jones DK, Keverne EB, Matthews PM, Milner AD, Prescott M, Ragan I, Shattock R, StraussII, J. *Review of Research Using Non-Human Primates: Report of a Panel Chaired by Professor Sir Patrick Bateson FRS.* 2011. London: Biotechnology and Biological Sciences Research Council, Medical Research Council, and Wellcome Trust. https://wellcome.org/sites/default/files/wtvm052279_1.pdf.

Beauchamp TL. The Belmont Report. In Emanuel EJ, Grady C, Crouch RA, Lie RK, Miller FG, Wendler D, editors. *The Oxford Textbook of Clinical Research Ethics* (pp. 149–55). 2008. New York: Oxford University Press.

Birke L, Arluke A, Michael M. *The Sacrifice: How Scientific Experiments Transform Animals and People.* 2007. West Lafayette, IN: Purdue University Press.

Boodman E. Coronavirus vaccine clinical trial starting without usual animal data. STAT. 2020 Mar 11. https://bit.ly/3yhzPyO.

Bradley A, Mennie N, Bibby PA, Cassaday HJ. Some animals are more equal than others: Validation of a new scale to measure how attitudes to animals depend on species and human purpose of use. *PLOS ONE.* 2020 Jan;15(1): e0227948. https://doi.org/10.1371/journal.pone.0227948.

Brain/MINDS. Marmoset research. Website. 2021. https://brainminds.jp/en/ research/kind/marmoset-research-en.

Braithwaite VA, Huntingford FA. Fish and welfare: Do fish have the capacity for pain perception and suffering? *Animal Welfare.* 2004 Feb;13(S1):S87–92.

Brutcher RE. Effects of sleep disruption and quetiapine on cocaine abuse: The path to development of a monkey model of PTSD. Unpublished PhD thesis, Wake Forest University. 2013. https://wakespace.lib.wfu.edu/handle/10339/ 38531.

Can ÖE, D'Cruze N, Macdonald DW. Dealing in deadly pathogens: Taking stock of the legal trade in live wildlife and potential risks to human health. *Global Ecology and Conservation*. 2019 Jan;17:e00515. https://doi.org/10.1016/j.gecco.2018.e00515.

Canadian Council on Animal Care. Guide to the care and use of experimental animals. 1993. https://ccac.ca/Documents/Standards/Guidelines/Experimental_Animals_Vol1.pdf.

Candelaria EC. Almost 45 Alamogordo lab chimps were denied sanctuary in 2019. A federal judge just ruled that wasn't the right call. *Albuquerque Journal*. 2022 Dec 15. https://bit.ly/4dzZvqB.

Canadian Institutes of Health Research, Natural Sciences and Engineering Research Council of Canada, and Social Sciences and Humanities Research Council of Canada. *Tri-Council Policy Statement: Ethical conduct for research involving humans*. 2022. https://ethics.gc.ca/eng/policy-politique_tcps2-eptc2_2022.html.

Carbone L. *What Animals Want*. 2004. Oxford: Oxford University Press.

Carbone L. Chapter 11 – Euthanasia and laboratory animal welfare. In Bayne K, Turner PV, editors. *Laboratory Animal Welfare* (pp. 157–69). 2014. Boston, MA: Academic Press. www.sciencedirect.com/science/article/abs/pii/B9780123851031000117?via%3Dihub.

Chatfield K, Schroeder D, Guantai A, Bhatt K, Bukusi E, Adhiambo Odhiambo J, Cook J, Kimani J. Preventing ethics dumping: The challenges for Kenyan research ethics committees. *Research Ethics*. 2021 Jan;17(1): 23–44.

Chimpanzee Health Improvement, Maintenance, and Protection Act of 2000. Pub. L. No. 106-551, 114 Stat. 2752.

Civil Rights of Institutionalized Persons Act of 1980. Pub. L. No. 96-247, 42 USC § 1997 et seq.

Cohen J. Another HIV vaccine strategy fails in large-scale study. *Science*. 2020 Feb 3. https://bit.ly/3UPBu6c.

Colley C. Revealed : US allowing long-tailed macaque imports despite risk of disease. *Guardian*. 2023 Jan 8. https://bit.ly/3QZNJMp.

Collin NG, Cowey A, Latto R, Marzi C. The role of frontal eye-fields and superior colliculi in visual search and non-visual search in rhesus monkeys. *Behavioural Brain Research*. 1982 Feb;4(2):177–93.

Collins FS. NIH will no longer support biomedical research on chimpanzees. National Institutes of Health. 2015 Nov 17. https://bit.ly/3wIgoPg.

Conlee KM, Rowan AN. The case for phasing out experiments on primates. *Hastings Center Report*. 2012 Nov;42(s1):S31–34.

Cook DJ, Tymianski M. Nonhuman primate models of stroke for translational neuroprotection research. *Neurotherapeutics*. 2012 Apr;9:371–79.

Council for International Organizations of Medical Sciences. *International Ethical Guidelines for Health-Related Research Involving Humans*. 2016. Geneva. https://bit.ly/3WZUBx0.

Council of Europe. Explanatory Memorandum relating to the European Prison Rules. Revised European version of the Standard Minimum Rules for the Treatment of Prisoners. 1987. Strasbourg. https://rm.coe.int/16804f856c.

Council of Europe Committee of Ministers. Prison and Criminological Aspects of the Control of Transmissible Diseases Including Aids and Related Health Problems in Prison: Recommendation No. R (93) 6. 1995. https://rm.coe.int/09000016804d7777.

Crozier GK, Fenton A, Meynell L, Peña-Guzmán DM. Nonhuman, all too human: Toward developing policies for ethical chimera research. In Johnson LSM, Fenton A, Shriver A, editors. *Neuroethics and Nonhuman Animals* (pp. 205–19). 2020. Cham: Springer.

Cyranoski D. Chinese effort to clone gene-edited monkeys kicks off. *Nature*. 2019 Feb;566(7742):15–17.

De Waal FB, Preston SD. Mammalian empathy: Behavioural manifestations and neural basis. *Nature Reviews Neuroscience*. 2017 Aug;18(8):498–509.

Diamond MC. Response of the brain to enrichment. *Anais da Academia Brasileira de Ciências*. 2001 Jun;73(2):211–20.

Engber D. In the summer of 1965, a female Dalmatian was stolen from a farm in Pennsylvania. Her story changed America. *Slate Magazine*. 2009 Dec 22. https://bit.ly/3Klga3H.

European Commission. Directive 2010/63/EU of the European Parliament and of the Council of 22 September 2010 on the protection of animals used for scientific purposes. EUR-Lex. 2010. https://eur-lex.europa.eu/legal-content/EN/TXT/?uri=CELEX:32010L0063.

European Commission. Scientific Committee on Health and Environment Risks (SCHER). The need for non-human primates in biomedical research, production and testing of products and devices. 2017. https://tinyurl.com/47bwz82h.

Faunalytics. Technological lock-in on laboratory animal research. Faunalytics. 2008 Jan 3. https://bit.ly/3VfxjBU.

FDA Modernization Act 2.0 of 2022. 21 USC 355, S. 5002.

Fenton A. Can a chimp say "no"?: Reenvisioning chimpanzee dissent in harmful research. *Cambridge Quarterly of Healthcare Ethics*. 2014 Apr;23(2):130–39.

Fenton A. Holding animal-based research to our highest ethical standards: Re-seeing two emergent laboratory practices and the ethical significance of research animal dissent. *ILAR Journal.* 2019 Jul;60(3):397–403.

Fenton A, Johnson LSM. COVID-19 animal research reveals ethical shortcomings. *Impact Ethics.* 2020 Sep 25. https://bit.ly/4aDwkAf.

Ferdowsian H, Fuentes A. Harms and deprivation of benefits for nonhuman primates in research. *Theoretical Medicine and Bioethics.* 2014 Apr;35: 143–56.

Ferdowsian H, Johnson LSM. Primates in medical research: A matter of convenience, not sound science. The Hastings Center Bioethics Forum. 2022 Jul 8. https://bit.ly/3wQDzqu.

Ferdowsian H, Fuentes A, Johnson LSM, King BJ, Pierce J. Toward an anti-maleficent research agenda. *Cambridge Quarterly of Healthcare Ethics.* 2022 Jan;31(1):54–58.

Ferdowsian H, Johnson LSM, Johnson J, Fenton A, Shriver A, Gluck J. A Belmont Report for animals? *Cambridge Quarterly of Healthcare Ethics.* 2020 Jan;29(1):19–37.

Fernandez-Duque E, Huck M, Van Belle S, Di Fiore A. The evolution of pair-living, sexual monogamy, and cooperative infant care: Insights from research on wild owl monkeys, titis, sakis, and tamarins. *American Journal of Physical Anthropology.* 2020 May;171:118–73.

Fernström AL, Sutian W, Royo F, Fernström AL, Sutian W, Royo F, Westlund K, Nilsson T, Carlsson HE, Paramastri Y, Pamungkas J. Stress in cynomolgus monkeys (*Macaca fascicularis*) subjected to long-distance transport and simulated transport housing conditions. *Stress.* 2008 Jan;11 (6):467–76.

Frank J. Technological lock-in, positive institutional feedback, and research on laboratory animals. *Structural Change and Economic Dynamics.* 2005;16 (4):557–75.

Gamillo E. All animals are accounted for after truck carrying 100 lab monkeys crashed in Pennsylvania. *Smithsonian Magazine.* 2022 Jan 26. https://bit.ly/ 3yu1LPS.

Garner JP. The significance of meaning: Why do over 90% of behavioral neuroscience results fail to translate to humans, and what can we do to fix it? ILAR *Journal.* 2014 Dec;55(3):438–56.

German Ethics Council. *Human–Animal Mixtures in Research.* 2011. Deutscher Ethikrat, Berlin. https://bit.ly/4c0ivg8.

Goldby S. Experiments at the Willowbrook State School. *The Lancet.* 1971 Apr;297(7702):749.

Gosepath S. Equality. *Stanford Encyclopedia of Philosophy.* 2021. https://plato.stanford.edu/entries/equality/.

Greely HT, Cho MK, Hogle LF, Satz DM. Thinking about the human neuron mouse. *American Journal of Bioethics.* 2007 May;7(5):27–40.

Griffith RW, Humphrey DR. Long-term gliosis around chronically implanted platinum electrodes in the Rhesus macaque motor cortex. *Neuroscience Letters.* 2006 Oct;406(1–2):81–86.

Grimm D. Decision to end monkey experiments based on finances, not animal rights, NIH says. *Science.* 2015 Dec 14. https://bit.ly/3UZ1coR.

Grimm D. U.S. labs using a record number of monkeys. *Science.* 2018 Nov;362(6415):630.

Grimm D. NIH hosts nonhuman primate workshop amidst increased scrutiny of monkey research. *Science.* 2020 Feb 20. https://bit.ly/4bvUuxJ.

Grimm D. Harvard studies on infant monkeys draw fire, split scientists. *Science.* 2022a Oct 19. https://bit.ly/3Kh3r1J.

Grimm D. Indictment of monkey importers could disrupt US research. *Science.* 2022b Dec;378(6623):934–35.

Grimm D. US, European researchers face monkey shortage crisis. *Science.* 2023;380(6645):567–68.

Gudakunst DW. Letter from Gudakunst, Don W. to Sabin, Albert B. dated 1940-12-05. University of Cincinnati. Hauck Center for the Albert B. Sabin Archives. https://drc.libraries.uc.edu/handle/2374.UC/691513

Hamzelou J. This company plans to transplant gene-edited pig hearts into babies next year. *MIT Technology Review.* 2023 Jul 17. https://bit.ly/4bKsK8i.

Hansen MF, Gill M, Nawangsari VA, Sanchez KL, Cheyne SM, Nijman V, Fuentes A. Conservation of long-tailed macaques: Implications of the updated IUCN status and the COVID-19 pandemic. *Primate Conservation.* 2021 Jan;35:1.

Hansen M, Ang A, Trinh T, Sy E, Paramasivam S, Ahmed T, Dimalibot J, Jones-Engel L, Ruppert N, Griffioen C, Lwin N, Phiapalath P, Gray R, Kite S, Doak N, Nijman V, Fuentes A, Gumert MD. *Macaca fascicularis.* The IUCN Red List of Threatened Species. 2022a: e.T12551A199563077. https://dx.doi.org/10.2305/IUCN.UK.2022-1.RLTS.T12551A199563077.en.

Hansen MF, Gill M, Briefer EF, Nielsen DR, Nijman V. Monetary value of live trade in a commonly traded primate, the long-tailed macaque, based on global trade statistics. *Frontiers in Conservation Science.* 2022b Feb; 3:16.

Harlow HF, Suomi SJ. Induced depression in monkeys. *Behavioral Biology.* 1974 Nov;12(3):273–96.

Hartung T. A toxicology for the 21st century: Mapping the road ahead. *Toxicological Sciences.* 2009 May;109(1):18–23.

Hawthorne WJ, Salvaris EJ, Chew YV, Burns H, Hawkes J, Barlow H, Hu M, Lew AM, Nottle MB, O'Connell PJ, Cowan PJ. Xenotransplantation of genetically modified neonatal pig islets cures diabetes in baboons. *Frontiers in Immunology.* 2022 Jun;13:898948.

Hayward A, Sjoblom E, Sinclair S, Cidro J. A new era of indigenous research: Community-based indigenous research ethics protocols in Canada. *Journal of Empirical Research on Human Research Ethics.* 2021 Oct;16(4):403–17.

Herrmann K, Pistollato F, Stephens ML. Beyond the 3Rs: Expanding the use of human-relevant replacement methods in biomedical research. *ALTEX-Alternatives to animal experimentation.* 2019 Jul;36(3):343–52.

Imanis Life Sciences. Rochester's Vyriad developing oral COVID-19 vaccine. Imanis Life Sciences. 2021 Feb 25. https://imanislife.com/news/rochesters-vyriad-developing-oral-covid-19-vaccine/.

Institute of Medicine (US) and National Research Council (US) Committee on the Use of Chimpanzees in Biomedical and Behavioral Research. *Chimpanzees in Biomedical and Behavioral Research: Assessing the Necessity.* Altevogt BM, Pankevich DE, Shelton-Davenport MK, Kahn JP, editors. 2011. Washington, DC: National Academies Press. www.ncbi.nlm.nih.gov/books/NBK91445/.

Iritani S, Torii Y, Habuchi C, Sekiguchi H, Fujishiro H, Yoshida M, Go Y, Iriki A, Isoda M, Ozaki N. The neuropathological investigation of the brain in a monkey model of autism spectrum disorder with ABCA13 deletion. *International Journal of Developmental Neuroscience.* 2018 Dec;71:130–39.

Jacobs B. The neural cruelty of captivity: Keeping large mammals in zoos and aquariums damages their brains. *The Conversation.* 2020a Sep 24. https://bit.ly/44XvHjy.

Jacobs B. Keeping large mammals captive damages their brains. *EcoWatch.* 2020b Sep 30. www.ecowatch.com/animals-captivity-brain-damage-2647869196.html.

Johnson LSM. The road not mapped: The neuroethics roadmap on research with nonhuman primates. *AJOB Neuroscience.* 2020a Jul;11(3):176–83.

Johnson LSM. The trouble with nonhuman animals in brain research. In Johnson LSM, Fenton A, Shriver A, editors. *Neuroethics and Nonhuman Animals* (pp. 271–86). 2020b. Cham: Springer.

Johnson LSM. Interrogating the culture of human exceptionalism: Animal research and the neuroethics of animal minds and brains. In Farisco M, editor. *Neuroethics and Cultural Diversity* (pp. 249–70). 2023. London: ISTE Science/Wiley.

Jonsen AR. Nontherapeutic research with children: The Ramsey versus McCormick debate. *Journal of Pediatrics*. 2006 Jul;149(1):S12–14.

Kaas JH, Qi HX. The reorganization of the motor system in primates after the loss of a limb. *Restorative Neurology and Neuroscience*. 2004 Jan;22(3–5): 145–52.

Kandárová H, Letašiová S. Alternative methods in toxicology: Pre-validated and validated methods. *Interdisciplinary Toxicology*. 2011 Sep;4(3):107.

Kevany S, Colley C. Fate of 1,000 trafficked lab monkeys at center of US investigation in limbo. *Guardian*. 2023 Mar 20. https://bit.ly/3wImlM6.

King, BJ. What do we owe lab animals? *New York Times*. 2023 Jan 23. www.nytimes.com/2023/01/23/science/what-do-we-owe-lab-animals.html.

King, BJ. Plight of baby lab monkeys reaches Congress. *NPR*. 2015 Jan 29. https://bit.ly/3R2Nmk2.

Kinter LB, DeHaven R, Johnson DK, DeGeorge JJ. A brief history of use of animals in biomedical research and perspective on non-animal alternatives. *ILAR Journal*. 2021 Dec;62(1-2):7–16.

Kishi N, Sato K, Sasaki E, Okano H. Common marmoset as a new model animal for neuroscience research and genome editing technology. *Development, Growth & Differentiation*. 2014 Jan;56(1):53–62.

Knight A. The poor contribution of chimpanzee experiments to biomedical progress. *Journal of Applied Animal Welfare Science*. 2007 Sep;10(4): 281–308.

Krugman S. The Willowbrook hepatitis studies revisited: Ethical aspects. *Reviews of Infectious Diseases*. 1986 Jan;8(1):157–62.

Last1000chimps.com. Website. 2021. https://last1000chimps.com.

Leblanc M, Berry K, McCort H, Reuter JD. Brain abscess in a rhesus macaque (*Macaca mulatta*) with a cephalic implant. *Comparative Medicine*. 2013 Aug;63(4):367–72.

Levenson M. Monkeys escape after truck crashes on Pennsylvania highway. *Seattle Times*. 2022 Jan 21. https://bit.ly/4dVCUEO.

Liu Z, Cai Y, Liao Z, Xu Y, Wang Y, Wang Z, Jiang X, Li Y, Lu Y, Nie Y, Zhang X. Cloning of a gene-edited macaque monkey by somatic cell nuclear transfer. *National Science Review*. 2019 Jan;6(1):101–08.

Lohse S. Scientific inertia in animal-based research in biomedicine. *Studies in History and Philosophy of Science Part A*. 2021 Oct 1;89:41–51.

London AJ. *For the Common Good: Philosophical Foundations of Research Ethics*. 2021. New York: Oxford University Press.

Maldonado AM, Peck MR. Research and in situ conservation of owl monkeys enhances environmental law enforcement at the Colombian–Peruvian border. *American Journal of Primatology*. 2014 Jul;76(7):658–69.

Malisow C. What's to be the fate of 1,000 lab monkeys: Back to Cambodia, a new home in South Texas, or death? *Houston Press.* 2023 Mar 22. https://bit.ly/3KtOPfS.

Marthas ML, Van Rompay KK, Abbott Z, Earl P, Buonocore-Buzzelli L, Moss B, Rose NF, Rose JK, Kozlowski PA, Abel K. Partial efficacy of a VSV-SIV/MVA-SIV vaccine regimen against oral SIV challenge in infant macaques. *Vaccine.* 2011 Apr;29(17):3124–37.

Maxwell N. 35 chimpanzees living at the Alamogordo Primate Facility, down from 44 in 2019. *Alamogordo Daily News.* 2022 Mar 25. https://bit.ly/4aCTPck.

McManus R. Ex-director Zerhouni surveys value of NIH research. *NIH Record.* 2013 Jun;65(13):6–7.

Miller D. Justice. *Stanford Encyclopedia of Philosophy.* 2021. https://plato.stanford.edu/entries/justice/.

Moll J, Oliveira-Souza RD, Garrido GJ, Bramati IE, Caparelli-Daquer EM, Paiva ML, Zahn R, Grafman J. The self as a moral agent: Linking the neural bases of social agency and moral sensitivity. *Social Neuroscience.* 2007 Sep;2(3–4):336–52.

National Academies of Sciences, Engineering, and Medicine. *Nonhuman Primate Models in Biomedical Research: State of the Science and Future Needs.* 2023. Ramos KS, editor. Washington, DC: National Academies Press. https://doi.org/10.17226/26857.

National Centre for the Replacement, Refinement & Reduction of Animals in Research. The 3Rs. Website. 2017. www.nc3rs.org.uk/who-we-are/3rs.

National Commission for the Protection of Human Subjects of Biomedical and Behavioral Research. *The Belmont Report: Ethical Principles and Guidelines for the Protection of Human Subjects of Research.* 1979. Washington, DC: US Government Printing Office.

National Institute of Neurological Disorders and Stroke. Tissue plasminogen activator for acute ischemic stroke (Alteplase, Activase®). Website. 2014. https://bit.ly/4bPtZnf.

National Institutes of Health. *Council of Councils Working Group on the Use of Chimpanzees in NIH-Supported Research.* 2013. https://dpcpsi.nih.gov/council/pdf/FNL_Report_WG_Chimpanzees.pdf.

National Institutes of Health. Funding opportunities: Marmoset Coordination Center (U24 clinical trials not allowed). 2019. https://grants.nih.gov/grants/guide/rfa-files/RFA-MH-25-116.html.

National Institutes of Health. The BRAIN Initiative and neuroethics: Enabling and enhancing neuroscience advances for society. 2020. https://bit.ly/3wRjSPx.

National Institutes of Health Veterinary Panel. Animals classified as "not recommended for relocation." 2019. https://bit.ly/3VpGCzh.

National Primate Research Centers. Website. https://nprcresearch.org/primate/.

National Research Council (US) Committee on Guidelines for the Humane Transportation of Laboratory Animals. *Guidelines for the Humane Transportation of Research Animals.* 2006. Washington, DC: National Academies Press. www.ncbi.nlm.nih.gov/books/NBK19637/.

National Research Council (US) Committee on Long-Term Care of Chimpanzees. *Chimpanzees in Research: Strategies for Their Ethical Care, Management, and Use.* 1997. Washington, DC: National Academies Press. www.ncbi.nlm.nih.gov/books/NBK109746/.

National Toxicology Program. Alternative methods accepted by US agencies. Website. 2024. https://ntp.niehs.nih.gov/whatwestudy/niceatm/accept-methods.

Nature Magazine. Editorial: *Nature* addresses helicopter research and ethics dumping. *Nature.* 2022 May;606(7912):7. www.nature.com/articles/d41586-022-01423-6.

Neergaard L. Solving "the next public health crisis" is being undermined by a shortage of monkeys, panel controversially concludes. *Fortune.* 2023 May 4. https://fortune.com/2023/05/04/research-monkey-shortage-medical-biomedical-testing/.

New England Primate Conservancy. Primates in animal studies. Website. 2021. https://neprimateconservancy.org/primates-in-animal-studies/.

Novak MA, Hamel AF, Kelly BJ, Dettmer AM, Meyer JS. Stress, the HPA axis, and nonhuman primate well-being: A review. *Applied Animal Behaviour Science.* 2013 Jan;143(2-4):135–49.

O'Collins VE, Macleod MR, Donnan GA, Horky LL, Van Der Worp BH, Howells DW. 1,026 experimental treatments in acute stroke. *Annals of Neurology.* 2006 Mar;59(3):467–77.

O'Dell R. Monkey farm under fire for more primate deaths at its Mesa facility. *Arizona Republic.* 2022 Aug 17. https://bit.ly/4dV9tTs.

Offit PA. *Vaccinated: One Man's Quest to Defeat the World's Deadliest Diseases.* 2007. New York: Smithsonian Books/Collins.

Oikonomidis L, Santangelo AM, Shiba Y, Clarke FH, Robbins TW, Roberts AC. A dimensional approach to modeling symptoms of neuropsychiatric disorders in the marmoset monkey. *Developmental Neurobiology.* 2017 Mar;77(3):328–53.

Owens B. Canada used hungry indigenous children to study malnutrition. *Nature.* 2013 Jul 23. https://doi.org/10.1038/nature.2013.13425.

Pamies D, Hartung T. 21st century cell culture for 21st century toxicology. *Chemical Research in Toxicology.* 2017 Jan;30(1):43–52.

Peat S. A search for answers in ethics: Where animals fit in. *UNM Newsroom.* 2023 Feb 14. https://news.unm.edu/news/a-search-for-answers-in-ethics-where-animals-fit-in.

Perreault S. Victimization of First Nations people, Métis and Inuit in Canada. Statistics Canada. 2022 Jul 19. www150.statcan.gc.ca/n1/pub/85-002-x/2022001/article/00012-eng.htm.

Phillips N. University of Wisconsin to reprise controversial monkey studies. *Wisconsin Watch.* 2014 Jul 31. https://bit.ly/4e8C5ZE.

Pluchino S, Gritti A, Blezer E, Amadio S, Brambilla E, Borsellino G, Cossetti C, Del Carro U, Comi G, 't Hart B, Vescovi A. Human neural stem cells ameliorate autoimmune encephalomyelitis in non-human primates. *Annals of Neurology: Official Journal of the American Neurological Association and the Child Neurology Society.* 2009 Sep;66(3):343–54.

Poirier C, Bateson M. Pacing stereotypies in laboratory rhesus macaques: Implications for animal welfare and the validity of neuroscientific findings. *Neuroscience & Biobehavioral Reviews.* 2017 Dec;83:508–15.

Pomerantz O, Meiri S, Terkel J. Socio-ecological factors correlate with levels of stereotypic behavior in zoo-housed primates. *Behavioural Processes.* 2013 Sep;98:85–91.

Pound P, Ebrahim S, Sandercock P, Bracken MB, Roberts I. Where is the evidence that animal research benefits humans? *BMJ.* 2004 Feb;328(7438): 514–17.

Qi HX, Stepniewska I, Kaas JH. Reorganization of primary motor cortex in adult macaque monkeys with long-standing amputations. *Journal of Neurophysiology.* 2000 Oct;84(4):2133–47.

Rachels J, Rachels S. *The Elements of Moral Philosophy.* 1986. Philadelphia, PA: Temple University Press.

Ramsey P. *The Patient as Person: Explorations in Medical Ethics*, 2nd ed. 2002. New Haven, CT: Yale University Press.

Rasmussen KL, Reite M. Loss-induced depression in an adult macaque monkey. *American Journal of Psychiatry.* 1982 May.

Reardon S. NIH modifies but still defends experiments on monkeys. *Scientific American.* 2015 Jan 29. https://bit.ly/4e4MvcG.

Reardon S. US lawmakers propose plan to reduce primate research at National Institutes of Health. *Nature.* 2019 May 9. https://bit.ly/3yEasqU.

Redmond, Jr DE. Using monkeys to understand and cure Parkinson disease. *Hastings Center Report.* 2012 Nov;42(s1):S7–11.

Reinhardt V, Liss C, Stevens C. Restraint methods of laboratory non-human primates: A critical review. *Animal Welfare*. 1995 Aug;4(3):221–38.

Resnik DB. Compensation for research-related injuries, ethical and legal issues. *Journal of Legal Medicine*. 2006 Sep;27(3):263–87.

Robinson WM, Unruh BT. The hepatitis experiments at the Willowbrook State School. In Emanuel EJ, Grady CC, Crouch RA, Lie RK, Miller FG, Wendler DD, editors. *The Oxford Textbook of Clinical Research Ethics* (pp. 80–85). 2008. Oxford: Oxford University Press.

Robitzski D. What happens to science when model organisms become endangered? *Scientist Magazine*. 2022 Oct 13. https://bit.ly/3yBHSqh.

Rollin BE. The moral status of animals and their use as experimental subjects. In Kuhse H, Singer P, editors. *A Companion to Bioethics* (pp. 495–509). 2009. Oxford: Wiley-Blackwell.

Rush ER, Dale E, Aguirre AA. Illegal wildlife trade and emerging infectious diseases: Pervasive impacts to species, ecosystems and human health. *Animals*. 2021 Jun;11(6):1821.

Russell WM, Burch RL. *The Principles of Humane Experimental Technique*. 1959. London: Methuen.

Safer Medicines. Breaking the lock-in to animal research within academia. Website. 2021. https://safermedicines.org/breaking-the-lock-in-to-animal-research-within-academia/.

SC Johnson. SC Johnson point of view on animal testing. 2019 Oct 23. www.scjohnson.com/en/newsroom/statements/sc-johnson-point-of-view-on-animal-testing.

Schecter A. The fate of 1,000 research monkeys is unclear after government intervention. *NBC News*. 2023 Mar 16. https://bit.ly/3wQkDs2.

Schroeder D. Ethics dumping: The exploitative side of academic research. *Guardian*. 2018 Aug 31. https://bit.ly/3QYChAH.

Schroeder D. What is ethics dumping? *Biologist*. 2019 Jun;66(3):2–25. https://thebiologist.rsb.org.uk/biologist-features/what-is-ethics-dumping.

Schroeder D, Cook J, Hirsch F, Fenet S, Muthuswamy V. *Ethics Dumping: Case Studies from North–South Research Collaborations*. 2018. Cham: Springer Nature.

Schwarz DA, Lebedev MA, Hanson TL, Dimitrov DF, Lehew G, Meloy J, Rajangam S, Subramanian V, Ifft PJ, Li Z, Ramakrishnan A. Chronic, wireless recordings of large-scale brain activity in freely moving rhesus monkeys. *Nature Methods*. 2014 Jun;11(6):670–76.

Sekaly RP. The failed HIV Merck vaccine study: A step back or a launching point for future vaccine development? *Journal of Experimental Medicine*. 2008 Jan;205(1):7–12.

Shanks N, Greek R. Experimental use of nonhuman primates is not a simple problem. *Nature Medicine*. 2008 Oct;14(10):1012.

Shapiro R, Schecter A, Lehren A, Delgado A. How the race for a Covid vaccine enriched monkey poachers and endangered macaques. *NBC News*. 2022 Dec 17. https://bit.ly/3UXJ1zY.

Shook C. Reevaluating the practice of animal testing in biomedical research. American Bar Association. 2022 Dec 28. https://bit.ly/3wVQrvx.

Smith AJ, Clutton RE, Lilley E, Hansen KEA, Brattelid T. PREPARE: Guidelines for planning animal research and testing. *Laboratory Animals*. 2018 Aug;52(2):135–41.

Smith JS. *Patenting the Sun*. 1990. New York: William Morrow.

Sneddon LU, Brown C. Mental capacities of fishes. In Johnson L, Fenton A, Shriver A, editors. *Neuroethics and Nonhuman Animals* (pp. 53–71). 2020. Cham: Springer.

Solis-Moreira J. SARS-CoV-2 antibody profiles in vaccinated and convalescent macaques compared to humans. *News Medical*. 2021 Dec 8. https://bit.ly/3KkuOYY.

Stanford Medicine. Why animal research? Website. 2023. https://med.stanford.edu/animalresearch/why-animal-research.html.

Suleman MA, Wango E, Sapolsky RM, Odongo H, Hau J. Physiologic manifestations of stress from capture and restraint of free-ranging male African green monkeys (*Cercopithecus aethiops*). *Journal of Zoo and Wildlife Medicine*. 2004 Mar;35(1):20–24.

Sun D. 90% of drugs fail clinical trials – here's one way researchers can select better drug candidates. *The Conversation*. 2022 Feb 23. https://bit.ly/4bBMYRQ.

Suntsova MV, Buzdin AA. Differences between human and chimpanzee genomes and their implications in gene expression, protein functions and biochemical properties of the two species. *BMC Genomics*. 2020 Sep21(7):535.

Suri T. Between simians and cell lines: Rhesus monkeys, polio research, and the geopolitics of tissue culture (1934–1954). *Journal of the History of Biology*. 2022 Mar;55(1):115–46.

The Humane Society of the United States et al. v. *National Institutes of Health et al.*, No. 8:2021cv00121 – Document 73 (D. Md. 2023). www.mdd.uscourts.gov/sites/mdd/files/21-121-LKG-Opinion.pdf.

Transportation, Sale, and Handling of Certain Animals of 2011. 7 USC Ch. 54. https://uscode.house.gov/view.xhtml?path=/prelim@title7/chapter54&edition=prelim.

Traystman RJ. Animal models of focal and global cerebral ischemia. *ILAR Journal*. 2003 Jan;44(2):85–95.

Turner PV. The history of chimpanzees in biomedical research. In Robinson LM, Weiss A, editors. *Nonhuman Primate Welfare* (pp. 31–55). 2023. Cham: Springer.

Tyson, L. Sanctuary is not the answer: Why legal change is the only way to end the suffering of monkeys. Born Free USA. https://www.bornfreeusa.org/2021/09/01/sanctuary-is-not-the-answer-why-legal-change-is-the-only-way-to-end-the-suffering-of-monkeys/

United Nations. Body of principles for the protection of all persons under any form of detention or imprisonment. OHCHR. 1988. https://bit.ly/3X2ahjl.

Urano E, Okamura T, Ono C, Ueno S, Nagata S, Kamada H, Higuchi M, Furukawa M, Kamitani W, Matsuura Y, Kawaoka Y. COVID-19 cynomolgus macaque model reflecting human COVID-19 pathological conditions. *Proceedings of the National Academy of Sciences*. 2021 Oct;118(43): e2104847118.

US Department of Agriculture (APHIS). APHIS Research Facility Annual Summary & Archive Reports. 2013. https://bit.ly/4bG9LvZ.

US Department of Agriculture (APHIS). Annual report animal usage by fiscal year (2019). 2021 Apr 27. https://bit.ly/4c0FZll.

US Department of Health and Human Services. Federal policy for the protection of human subjects. Website. 2009. www.hhs.gov/ohrp/regulations-and-policy/regulations/common-rule/index.html.

US Fish and Wildlife Service. 50 CFR Part 17 endangered and threatened wildlife and plants; listing all chimpanzees as endangered species. Federal Register, Vol. 80, No. 115. 2015.

US Government Accounting Office. Animal use in research: Federal agencies should assess and report on their efforts to develop and promote alternatives. Website. 2019 Sep 24. www.gao.gov/products/gao-19-629#:~:text=Recommendations.

Wang A, Yuan A. Researchers call on NIH to stop funding primate experiments at Harvard Medical School. *Harvard Crimson*. 2023 Feb 24. www.thecrimson.com/article/2023/2/24/letter-nih-monkey-research/.

Warne RK, Moloney GK, Chaber AL. Is biomedical research demand driving a monkey business? *One Health*. 2023 Jun;16:100520.

Watkins DI, Burton DR, Kallas EG, Moore JP, Koff WC. Nonhuman primate models and the failure of the Merck HIV-1 vaccine in humans. *Nature Medicine*. 2008 Jun;14(6):617–21.

Weatherall D, Goodfellow P, Harris J. The use of non-human primates in research: A working group report chaired by Sir David Weatherall. 2006. https://royalsociety.org/news-resources/publications/2006/weatherall-report/.

Weintraub K. A CRISPR startup is testing pig organs in monkeys to see if they're safe for us. *MIT Technology Review.* 2019 Jun 12. https://bit.ly/4bXQ6HJ.

Williams-Blangero S, VandeBerg JL, Dyke B. Genetic management of nonhuman primates. *Journal of Medical Primatology.* 2002 Feb;31(1):1–7.

Wisconsin National Primate Research Center. Wikipedia. 2023. https://en.wikipedia.org/wiki/Wisconsin_National_Primate_Research_Center.

World Medical Association. Declaration of Helsinki – Ethical principles for medical research involving human subjects. Helsinki, 1964. https://bit.ly/3x3954K.

Xu SY, Pan SY. The failure of animal models of neuroprotection in acute ischemic stroke to translate to clinical efficacy. *Medical Science Monitor Basic Research.* 2013 Jan;19:37–45.

Zhang S. America is running low on a crucial resource for COVID-19 vaccines. *Atlantic.* 2020 Aug 31. www.theatlantic.com/science/archive/2020/08/america-facing-monkey-shortage/615799/.

Zhao H, Jiang YH, Zhang YQ. Modeling autism in non-human primates: Opportunities and challenges. *Autism Research.* 2018 May;11(5):686–94.

Acknowledgments

The National Anti-Vivisection Society (NAVS) extends its deepest gratitude to the individuals whose commitment and contributions have created, enriched, and elevated this important work.

Special recognition is owed to to L. Syd M Johnson, PhD, Andrew Fenton, PhD, and Mary Lee Jensvold, PhD, who, as core authors, dedicated countless hours to the drafting, reviewing, and editing process. They played pivotal roles in shaping the narrative, ensuring coherence, and upholding the highest standards of scholarly inquiry. Their collective expertise, commitment to ethical inquiry, and passion for the subject matter have been instrumental in bringing this manuscript to fruition.

We are grateful for the participation of Lori Marino, PhD and Kathrin Herrmann, PhD in our initial panel discussions. Their contributions to those discussions greatly informed the development of this Element. We extend our thanks to Barbara J. King for her moving contribution.

We wouldn't be able to advance the NAVS mission without the dedicated staff who devote their time and talents across our programs to transform science education and scientific research and support animals in need. Special thanks go to Kenneth Kandaras, Juliane Pearson, Pamela Osenkowski, Meredith Blanchard, and Anna Madsen for their contributions to this Element.

We express our sincere appreciation to the many reviewers who generously dedicated their time and expertise to scrutinize and refine this work. Their thoughtful insights and constructive feedback significantly enhanced the quality and rigor of our exploration into the use of nonhuman primates in research. We especially thank Matthew Altman, Christine Buckmaster, Maneesha Deckha, Hope Ferdowsian, Simon Gadbois, Gilly Griffin, Lori Gruen, Amy Kerwin, Barbara J. King, Elisabeth Ormandy, Pandora Pound, Toolika Rastogi, Jeff Sebo, Marty Stephens, Robert Streiffer, and Michael Walker for their help.

We are grateful to the Carroll Petrie Foundation, whose grant supported the development of this Element.

Finally, and most importantly, NAVS would like to extend its gratitude to our supporters, without whom this work would not be possible. Since 1929, NAVS has worked to end the exploitation of animals in the name of science. Thanks to the unwavering support of our donors and animal advocates, NAVS can continue its work to advance science to benefit humans and nonhuman animals.

The authors additionally thank the members of the Harvard Yale Animal Ethics faculty seminar for their helpful discussion of an early version. Andrew Fenton extends his personal thanks to colleagues at the Canadian Council on Animal Care (CCAC), from whom he learned much while serving on the organization's subcommittee that revised its core ethics document.

Cambridge Elements

Bioethics and Neuroethics

Thomasine Kushner

California Pacific Medical Center, San Francisco

Thomasine Kushner, PhD, is the founding Editor of the *Cambridge Quarterly of Healthcare Ethics* and coordinates the International Bioethics Retreat, where bioethicists share their current research projects, the Cambridge Consortium for Bioethics Education, a growing network of global bioethics educators, and the Cambridge-ICM Neuroethics Network, which provides a setting for leading brain scientists and ethicists to learn from each other.

About the Series

Bioethics and neuroethics play pivotal roles in today's debates in philosophy, science, law, and health policy. With the rapid growth of scientific and technological advances, their importance will only increase. This series provides focused and comprehensive coverage in both disciplines consisting of foundational topics, current subjects under discussion and views toward future developments.

Cambridge Elements ≡

Bioethics and Neuroethics

Elements in the Series

Pathographies of Mental Illness
Nathan Carlin

Immune Ethics
Walter Glannon

What Placebos Teach Us about Health and Care: A Philosopher Pops a Pill
Dien Ho

The Methods of Neuroethics
Luca Malatesti and John McMillan

Antinatalism, Extinction, and the End of Procreative Self-Corruption
Matti Häyry and Amanda Sukenick

Philosophical, Medical, and Legal Controversies About Brain Death
L. Syd M Johnson

Conscientious Objection in Medicine
Mark Wicclair

Art and Artificial Intelligence
Göran Hermerén

One Health Environmentalism
Benjamin Capps

Euthanasia as Privileged Compassion
Martin Buijsen

Capacity, Informed Consent and Third-Party Decision-Making
Jacob M. Appel

The Three Pillars of Ethical Research with Nonhuman Primates: A Work Developed in Collaboration with the National Anti-Vivisection Society
L. Syd M Johnson, Andrew Fenton and Mary Lee Jensvold

A full series listing is available at: www.cambridge.org/EBAN